# INSIG

# FLORIDA KEYS

*GREAT LITTLE GUIDES*

*Compact Guide: Florida Keys* is the ideal quick-reference guide to this fascinating corner of the USA, exploring its culture and its history, the splendors of the beaches and the wealth of the wildlife, as well as the delights of idiosyncratic Key West.

This is one of more than 80 titles in *Apa Publications'* new series of pocket-sized, easy-to-use guidebooks intended for the independent-minded traveler. *Compact Guides* are in essence travel encyclopedias in miniature, designed to be comprehensive yet portable, as well as up-to-date and authoritative.

MW00737813

## Star Attractions

An instant reference to some of Florida Keys' top attractions to help you set your priorities.

*The African Queen p19*

*John Pennekamp Reef State Park p20*

*Christ of the Deep p21*

*Dolphin Research Center p26*

*Mallory Square entertainer p40*

*Mel Fisher Maritime Museum p 41*

*Hemingway House p58*

*Southernmost Point p44*

*Dolphin Research Center p26*

*Captain Tony's Saloon p44*

*Fort Jefferson p51*

# FLORIDa Keys

## Introduction

## Places

## Culture

## Leisure

## Practical Information

# Florida Keys – The End of the Road

As the geographical tail of the US, the Florida Keys are indeed the end of the road. Casual and funky, uninhibited and hip, the chain of islands that makes up the Keys is a Mecca for misfits and free-spirited romantics.

*Rum Runners Bar*

A sultry wilderness graced with emerald green hammocks, blinding white beaches, pink flamingos, the bluest of blue waters, and balmy air redolent of sea salt, the Keys exude the spirit of the tropics and have a particular, sensual charm that is quick to captivate the senses.

In the early evenings, the bright tangerine sun slips gently into the sea and the night is usually welcomed with a toast in a cool glass of tequila. Soon afterwards, ramshackle saloons fill up with weather-beaten boat skippers who blend in with the weather-beaten decor.

Although blemished by tourist development, the Keys still offer a soothing sanctuary from the intensity of modern urban life, and are without a doubt one of America's unmissable destinations.

**5**

## History

A thousand years ago the rocky landscape of Florida Keys was inhabited by Caloosa Indians. According to archeologists, they established a fairly sophisticated society. Archeological digs have uncovered evidence of primitive crop cultivation, red clay cooking utensils, and huge burial mounds to honor tribal chiefs. But the Indians' lives were radically changed by the arrival of the Spanish in the 16th century.

*Tarot reader in Key West*

Juan Ponce de León discovered the Keys in 1513 and christened them 'Los Martires' – The Martyrs – because he thought they resembled a row of twisted and tortured men. He was followed, later in the century, by other Spanish explorers, who gave Key West the name 'Cayo Hueso' – Island of Bones – because of the mounds of bones they discovered there. Many of the Caloosa were killed fighting for their lands, others were enslaved, and some died of diseases borne by the European sailors.

During the 17th century British settlers from the Bahamas fished the waters off the Keys and initiated the unsavory business of wrecking. Lanterns strung in trees would lure ships onto the rocks, whereupon the wreckers would salvage the sinking cargo. Many unscrupulous people grew rich in this way, until lighthouses and reef warning buoys were established in the mid-19th century. A museum in Key West tells the whole story.

In 1821 Spain ceded Florida to the United States,

*Flying the flag*

*Lazy living*

*Taking the plunge*

and the first group of permanent settlers arrived – British Loyalists who had fled to the Bahamas during the American Revolution. They were known as Conchs (*see page 8*) and they soon made themselves at home. In 1845 Florida became the twenty-seventh state in the Union and two decades later supported the Confederate South in the Civil War.

During the 1880s the American government invested millions in the country's economy and Key West became a boom town. By 1890 it was the largest city in Florida and the wealthiest, per capita, in the United States. The economy of the Keys flourished.

In the days before people realised the grave damage that could be done by depleting natural resources, sponging was one of the biggest industries, for a while providing 90 percent of all natural sponges used in the US. Cigar making, a business run by Cuban settlers, was another lucrative industry, with some of the Key West cigars considered better than those that came from Havana.

There was a strong Cuban influence in the Keys during the late 18th century. It was here that José Martí, writer and patriot, plotted the revolution that would lead to Cuba gaining independence from Spain in 1898. The San Carlos Institute in Key West was the activists' headquarters, as well as a thriving opera house.

Accessible from the rest of the United States only by boat, the Keys had enjoyed a splendid isolation. But when, between 1905 and 12, Henry M. Flagler built a railroad linking Key West and Miami, the Keys became more closely integrated with the rest of the US. Gradually the islands would come to depend on the revenue from tourists (*see the section on Population and economy on pages 8–9*).

## Location and layout

An archipelago dangling off the southern tip of the Florida peninsula, the Keys consist of 31 limestone islands. These islands, geologists say, are different in their land-forms and life-forms from any other part of the US Atlantic Coast. They were created during a time span of more than 100,000 years, and when the sea level dropped during the last Ice Age, these islands were left above sea level.

A scattering of over 800 tiny, uninhabited islands surround the Keys. To the south and east lies the Atlantic Ocean, where just a few miles offshore runs the warm ocean current known as the Gulf Stream. To the west of the Keys is Florida Bay and the calm Gulf of Mexico.

The only true tropical environment in the continental US, the Keys are connected by a series of 43 concrete bridges, their lengths spanning from 37 feet (11 meters) to 7 miles (11km). Down the center runs the Overseas Highway which is actually the southernmost end of US Highway 1. Known as 'the highway that goes to the sea,' the 126-mile (203-km) Overseas Highway is an incredible feat of engineering. It was completed in 1938, just three years after a hurricane had completely destroyed Flagler's Florida East Coast Railroad, which had linked the Keys to the mainland.

The Keys are divided into three general regions: the Upper Keys, Middle Keys and Lower Keys. Immediately south of Florida City, the first of many small green signs with white numbers called Mile Markers appears. As the name implies, they mark each mile along Overseas Highway. MM126 means there are 126 miles (203km) to Key West; the southernmost, MM0 marks the entrance to Key West. From Miami, it takes about one and a half hours to drive to the Upper Keys and about three hours to make it non-stop to Key West. By air, Key West is a 40-minute flight from Miami. Although there are no longer any air or sea links, Key West is just 90 miles (145km) from Cuba.

*Hats made to order*

*Happy retirement*

## Climate and when to go

Located in the subtropics, the Keys have a climate similar to that of the Caribbean islands. And as part of the so-called sunshine state, they live up to this reputation. Basically there two seasons, summer and winter, or wet and dry. Clear, sunny skies prevail most of the year except for the summer months when afternoon thunderstorms are common.

These massive mounds of thick clouds suddenly appear and drench the land in quick bursts. It is not un-

*Flea Market*

*Alexandrian Palm*

*Theater of the Sea*

common during these storms for one patch of beach to be totally drenched while another area just a mile away stays completely dry and sunny. The summer months do still have the cooling ocean breezes, which means that the temperatures in the Keys are usually more comfortable than in most of the more northerly parts of the state.

The summer months also bring lightning storms as well as rain. Lightning kills an average of 10 people a year in Florida – the highest total in the United States. And a typical Florida Keys' thunderstorm produces 50 to 100 lightning strikes every 15 minutes. The best thing to do is to stay indoors; if you are in a car, stay in it rather than running for shelter.

The humidity rate is generally very high and at times, especially in summer, the sweltering air feels like a mild steam bath. Average temperatures range from 62–80°F (16–26°C) from December through February, 72–87°F (22–30°C) from March through May, 77–95°F (25–35°C) from June through August, and 69–86°F (20–30°C) from September through November.

Hurricanes are taken very seriously in the Keys, and generally occur between June and October. In August 1992, Hurricane Andrew plowed through South Florida causing $20 billion in damages in the Miami area, but fortunately the Keys were not directly hit. The National Weather Service, based in Miami, monitors all storms brewing in the area and issues warnings to local communities. The storm hierarchy used by the Weather Service moves from tropical disturbance, to tropical depression, to tropical storm, and finally hurricane. Should a hurricane pose a threat to the Keys, local authorities might order an evacuation of the area. Evacuation routes and shelters are clearly marked by signs along the Overseas Highway.

The dry winter months are high season in the Keys, meaning that this is the most desirable, the most crowded and the most expensive time of year. Hotels are usually heavily booked during the winter months, so reservations are advisable. But the summer months are also a popular time in the Keys, especially for families, despite the heat and humidity. The off seasons, spring and fall, are less crowded and less expensive.

## Population and economy

Sparsely populated, the Florida Keys have about 80,000 permanent residents, 28,000 of whom live in Key West. In winter months that figure swells considerably, as many Northerners have vacation homes in the Keys. Locals who can trace their heritage back several generations call themselves Conchs (pronounced *konks*), named both for the early Bahamian settlers who came to the Keys and for the large marine mollusk that is such a delicacy that it is now an endangered species. A true Conch, it is said, is someone who was 'born on the rock' of Key West. In addition to the Conchs, the Keys have an interesting population mix, made up of retirees from the Northeast and Midwest, Cuban immigrants, writers, artists, gays, hard-working fishermen, former drug smugglers, US military employees, and lots of colorful characters who have run away from mundane lifestyles elsewhere.

*Conch shells for sale*

The people of the Keys have a definite island mentality. In April 1982, after the federal government set up roadblocks in an attempt to reduce drug traffic and cut down on illegal immigrants, the Conchs staged a public protest. They gathered in Mallory Square, hoisted a flag emblazoned with a conch shell, handed out passports and ceremoniously declared themselves inhabitants of the Conch Republic. The Keys residents were quick to point out that they were not in favor of drug trafficking or keen to increase the numbers of 'illegals' – they simply did not welcome intrusion from the federal authorities. Their protest lasted a week, and a mock form of it has become a popular annual event.

**9**

A majority of the residents of the Keys now work in the lucrative tourism industry, which accounts for about 90 percent of the area's economy. The Keys first began to attract tourists when Henry Flagler's railroad linked Key West with Miami at the beginning of this century. Their numbers increased in the pre-war years: in 1927 Pan American Airways began scheduled flights from Key West to Havana; shortly afterwards, Ernest Hemingway made Key West his winter home, which brought the place to people's attention, and at-

*Great egret in the*
*Wild Bird Center*

Key West shopping

Sightseeing by scooter

tracted a number of other writers. In 1938 the Overseas Highway was constructed, enabling people to drive here from Miami; and in the late 1940s and early 1950s President Harry Truman gave the Keys his seal of approval by spending his vacations at the Key West Little White House.

But tourist numbers were still relatively small. Now, the Keys attracts over 3 million visitors each year, 20 percent from foreign countries and the rest from the US. The tourism industry means not just luxury hotels, but fishing guides, craft vendors, street performers, and T-shirt shop owners as well. Local officials say that every dollar spent by a tourist turns over seven times as it moves through the economy.

### The natural environment

Tourism, however, also relies on the natural environment of the Keys and ironically is one of its worst enemies. Tourism development has been directly tied to the loss of wildlife, coral reef damage, threats to the limited water supply, depleted fish reserves, and the destruction of native flora. Declared a National Marine Sanctuary in 1990, the Keys are one of the most ecologically vulnerable areas in Florida – so much so that in 1996 the National Oceanic and Atmospheric Administration (NOAA) implemented a management plan in an attempt to protect and restore the local ecosystem.

Sitting on top of a bed of limestone rock, the Keys are flat, close-to-sea-level islands covered by rich vegetation. Much of this vegetation consists of mangroves, spidery-looking trees that grow in the brackish water created by the fresh waters of Florida Bay mixing with the salty waters of the Gulf of Mexico. Mangroves are a crucial element of the entire ecosystem of Florida.

They stabilize the shoreline, filter the water, and serve as a breeding ground for birds and animals.

Much of the plant life in the Keys came by way of the West Indies, carried over by strong winds or the waves and currents of the ocean. The rest of the plants were brought by settlers who no doubt thought they were doing something beneficial. One of these plants is the tall, scraggly Australian pine. Although they appear to blend in with the environment, these trees have upset the natural balance of the local ecosystem by crowding out other, native plants.

Manatees, the big, bulky mammals often called sea cows, were once prevalent in the Keys, but in recent years have dwindled in number as tourism development has destroyed their habitat. Boat propellers have slashed the backs of many, while others have been caught up in fishing nets and tackle, and strangled.

The large marine snail called the conch is everywhere in the Keys – on the local flag, the county seal, the football team uniforms, and on restaurant menus, but not where it belongs – in the sea. Although it once flourished in local waters, conchs just about disappeared in the 1980s, due to over-harvesting for food and souvenirs. Florida outlawed conch fishing in 1985, and a conch-rescue project was put into effect in the late 1980s, but so far the conch population has not bounced back. At one time it was estimated that over 1 million of these marine mollusks lived offshore, but today there only about 300,000. The Florida Marine Patrol severely penalizes the poachers they are able to catch, but very few are ever caught.

One creature that is not endangered and still thrives in the Keys is the mosquito. Although their numbers drop in the winter, they are a constant nuisance in the summer months. So are the tiny sandflies known locally as 'no-see-ums' which nibble on ankles in the evening, and the fire ants, tiny red ants that live in mounds of dirt and can cause terribly painful allergic reactions. Bug repellent sprays are the best defense, but these creatures are very resilient. Keep arms and legs covered up as much as possible in the evenings when mosquitoes and sandflies are most voracious.

*Conch Train* **11**

## Outdoor activities

The presence of bugs shouldn't deter you from outdoor activities, for this is where the Florida Keys really come into their own. Fishing, of couse, is the main event, but there is plenty more to do on land and sea – especially sea: the Keys are a paradise for windsurfing, sailing, diving, snorkeling and kayaking. For more details see the *Active Vacations* section on page 68.

*Enjoying the great outdoors*

# Historical Highlights

**AD1000** The indigenous Caloosa Indians inhabit southern Florida and the Keys.

**1498** Italian navigator and map-maker John Cabot, sailing under the British flag, creates a rudimentary map of Florida.

**1513** In the spring, Spanish conquistador Juan Ponce de León accidentally 'discovers' Florida while searching for the Fountain of Youth, and becomes the first white man to walk on Florida soil. He calls the string of rocky islands he finds 'Los Martires,' The Martyrs.

**mid-1500s** Spanish settlers enslave many of the Caloosa Indians living in the Keys. Others die after contracting infectious diseases imported from Europe.

**1586** English seafarer Francis Drake attacks northern Florida and for the next two centuries Britain, Spain and France fight for possession of the peninsula.

**1700s** English settlers from the nearby Bahama Islands fish the waters of the Keys and establish the dubious but lucrative business of salvaging ships wrecked offshore.

**1763–83** The British accept Florida from Spain in exchange for Havana; British plantations established; after the Revolutionary War, Britain trades Florida back to Spain in return for the Bahamas and Gibraltar.

**1821** Spain cedes Florida and the Keys to the US. Andrew Jackson becomes the first state governor.

**1822** The first permanent settlers, Bahamians nicknamed 'Conchs,' come to Key West and the US Navy Pirate Fleet is established to ward off invading pirate ships. Juan Salas, a Spaniard, sells Key West to American businessman John Simonton for $2,000.

**1825** Key West constructs its first lighthouse.

**1830s** The Caloosa Indian population of the Florida Keys becomes extinct. The 11-acre (4.5-hectare) island of Indian Key flourishes as a salvage station and botanist John James Audubon pays the island a visit.

**1845** Florida officially becomes a US state (the twenty-seventh).

**1846–76** Fort Jefferson, about 70 miles (112km) west of Key West, is built to protect the local shipping industry.

**1852–80** Six lighthouses are built in the Middle Keys to prevent ships from running aground.

**1855** Key West's population blossoms to 2,700.

**1860** Key West cigar industry booms with 100 million cigars per year being rolled in over 150 factories in the city.

**1861–65** The American Civil War takes it toll. Florida secedes from the Union and supports the Confederate South. By the end of the war, over 5,000 Floridians have died, and the state has suffered $20 million in damages.

**1871** The San Carlos Institute is founded in Key West to teach Cuban immigrants the language and customs of their new country, and to preserve the heritage of their homeland.

**1874** The US government surveys and plots the land of the Florida Keys to make way for homesteading.

**1880–90** The cigar and sponge-diving industries transform Key West into the richest city per capita in the US.

**1898** During the Spanish-American War, revolutionary supporters smuggle guns from Key West to Cuba.

**1905–12** Railroad magnate Henry M. Flagler brings the last section of his Florida East Coast Railroad from Miami to Key West. More settlers, and tourists, head for Key West.

**1906** A hurricane hits the Upper Keys, and more than 100 construction workers are killed when their barge is swept out to sea.

**1911** The original Seven-Mile Bridge, once called the Eighth Wonder of the World, opens.

**1919** During World War I, the US government passes the Prohibition law prohibiting the manufacture, sale and use of liquor. The Florida Keys become a haven for rum-smugglers throughout the 1920s.

**1927** Pan American World Airways is born and begins regularly scheduled flights from Key West to Havana, Cuba.

**1931–40** Author Ernest Hemingway makes Key West his winter home. Soon afterwards Key West becomes a fashionable tourist town.

**1934** The Key West Aquarium opens: the first commercial tourist attraction built in the Keys.

**1935** More than 800 people are killed in the Upper Keys when an unnamed hurricane slams ashore and blows the railroad to pieces.

**1938** The much awaited Overseas Highway, a 126-mile (203-km) road running from north of Key Largo all the way to Key West, replaces the Florida East Coast Railroad. Families, packed inside big American cars, begin driving to the tourist Mecca at the end of the road.

**1940s** The US Navy constructs a massive pipeline providing a much-needed supply of fresh water to the Keys.

**1946–53** President Harrry Truman vacations at the Key West Little White House.

**1948** Premier of the legendary film classic Key Largo, starring Humphrey Bogart and Lauren Bacall.

**1950s** Post-World War II exuberance means more and more tourists flock to Florida and the Keys.

**1953** Playwright Tennessee Williams adopts Key West as his home; a few years later numerous gays begin to migrate to the city

**1959** Fidel Castro takes control of Cuba,which triggers a decade-long influx of Cuban refugees to Key West, although most eventually move northward to Miami.

**1960** John Pennekamp Coral Reef State Park, the first underwater state park in the US, opens.

**1980** The Freedom Flotilla, a fleet of privately-owned US registered boats, carries 125,000 Cuban refugees released by President Castro from Cuba to the Key West harbor.

**1982** Angered over anti-drug smuggling roadblocks set up in the Keys, local residents stage a mock ceremony to secede from the state of Florida, and declare the Keys the 'Conch Republic.' In honor of this event, Key West now hosts an annual Conch Republic festival.

**1982** The new and improved Seven-Mile Bridge opens.

**1985** Key West salvage diver Mel Fisher and his crew recover the largest shipwreck treasure in the world off the Florida Keys, valued at about $4 billion.

**1990** The Florida Keys are designated a National Marine Sanctuary.

**1994** Economic hardship in Cuba, due to the break up of the Soviet Union, spawns another mass exodus of Cuban refugees, many of whom come ashore in the Florida Keys

### Hurricanes

Hurricanes are a part of 20th-century history in Florida. The one that slammed into the Upper Keys in 1935 didn't even have a name, but it blew the East Coast Railroad to pieces and killed more than 800 people.The Keys escaped the wrath of Hurricane Andrew which hit South Florida in 1992, leaving a trail of death and devastation. Winds of 160mph (255kph) and a 12-foot (3.5-meter) tidal wave destroyed over 60,000 homes and left 150,000 homeless, although the death toll was much lower than in 1935. Troops, joined by civilian volunteers and the Red Cross, helped to construct temporary accommodation and were assisted by foreign aid after images of the destruction appeared in the media, a cheering example of international co-operation.

*Key Largo boatyard*

*Key Largo, Highway 1*

## Tour 1

**Miami – ★★★ Key Largo – Tavernier** (65 miles/105 km) *See map below*

Heading south from Miami, the drive to the Keys is nothing less than spectacular – shimmering blue water on either side, the salty scent of the sea, and a natural light so bright it can actually strain the eyes. On the way there are vast fruit and vegetable fields, and many pockets of not-so-pretty shopping centers. Just south of **Florida City** (30 miles/48 km), where Hurricane Andrew wreaked havoc in 1992, US1 becomes the **Overseas Highway**, the busy artery that continues all the way to Key West. At this point there are two choices: the Overseas Highway direct to Key Largo, or **Card Sound Road**, a longer, more scenic toll

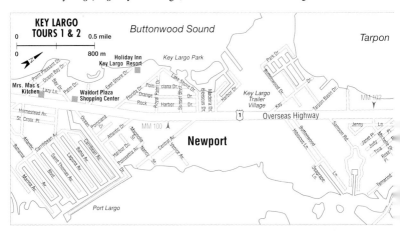

road that intersects with the Overseas Highway in North Key Largo at MM109.

Card Sound Road meanders past dense mangroves full of herons and egrets with a view of the **Turkey Point** nuclear power station in the distance. It also passes by **Alabama Jacks**, a popular restaurant and bar where country and western music blares constantly from the juke box.

*Key Largo souvenir*

Overseas Highway, completed in 1938, replaced the historic East Coast Railway which for decades was the only connection, except for boats, that the Florida Keys had to the rest of the state. On its east side is the Atlantic Ocean, on the west, the Gulf of Mexico. Just south of Florida City the first of many Mile Markers appears – MM126 – which means 126 miles (203km) from Key West. About 10 miles (16km) south of here is the eastern boundary of Monroe County, the south Florida county that contains the Keys, the Florida Everglades, and John Pennekamp Coral Reef State Park (*see Tour 2*).

The northernmost large community in the Keys is **Key Largo** (pop. 10,000), the town made famous by the movie from which it took its name. The **Key Largo Chamber of Commerce** (MM106) is a helpful place to stop for area information. Originally called Rock Harbor, this sleepy island town decided to capitalize on the romance and adventure associated with the 1948 Humphrey Bogart and Lauren Bacall film classic, and changed its name that same year. Although most of the film was shot on a soundstage in Hollywood, and Bogie and Bacall never once set foot in the Keys during the filming, Key Largo continues to flaunt the island's mythical allure.

A few minor scenes were in fact filmed in the town;

**17**

*Stop for information*

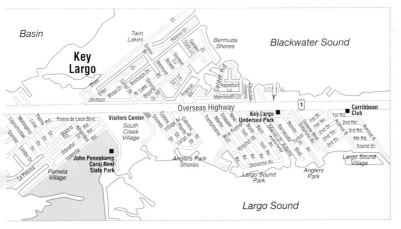

*The Caribbean Club*

*Joe Kimbell, Maritime Museum owner*

*Going down...*

one in particular was shot at the **Caribbean Club**, a former luxury hotel. Today, the Caribbean Club (MM104) is a drinking man's saloon open 24 hours a day, which brazenly brags about its movie history. Rebuilt when the original structure was destroyed in a fire, it has an old-fashioned tin roof and sweeping sunset views from the bar. Old movie posters and photos of Bogie and Bacall hang on the walls, paddle fans whir from above, and its pool table has been the cause of more than one drunken brawl. Although a bit rough around the edges, the Caribbean Club is a local hangout where tourists are warmly welcomed. More movie memorabilia can be found at the Holiday Inn Key Largo Resort (*see next page*).

One of the more natural assets of Key Largo is the **Key Largo Undersea Park** (daily 9am–3pm, tel: 451-2353) and **Jules' Undersea Lodge** (MM103.5). Located 22 feet (nearly 7 meters) below the surface of a lagoon, the Undersea Park is a family attraction with a marine archaeological exhibit to which you have to dive or snorkel. It also has underwater music, shipwrecks, lobster habitat exhibits, and artwork. The Undersea Lodge, a 30x50-foot (9x15-meter) concrete structure 30 feet (9 meters) under water, has self-contained private cabins that are available for rent. The cabins have telephones and televisions, and a view of fish and scuba divers who pass by.

At MM102 is the ★**Maritime Museum** (daily 10am–5pm, tel: 451-6444)). Throughout history, hundreds of ships have wrecked along the reefs of the Florida Keys, and this museum features fascinating exhibits of this legacy. Along with a reconstructed shipwreck and chronological displays, it has maritime artifacts spanning 400 years – gold medallions, silver bars, copper coins, pocket watches, antique charts and

cannons. It also has some artifacts from the *Henrietta Marie*, a British slave ship that sank off the Florida Keys in 1700, on its way to the West Indies. Carrying over 200 slaves, the *Henrietta Marie* was the only slave ship salvaged that was actually engaged in the trade at the time it sank. A few of the museum's historic pieces are for sale.

The ★★ **Holiday Inn Key Largo Resort** (MM100), has the original 30-foot (9-meter) boat from the movie *The African Queen* moored at the resort's marina. Used by Humphrey Bogart and Katherine Hepburn in the film, this steam-powered wooden craft regularly takes tourists on tours of the local waterways. Occasionally, the captain even takes a lifesize Humphrey Bogart dummy out for a ride too. Although the movie was filmed in England and Africa, and has no real relation to the Keys, the site of that old red boat with its canvas canopy brings a smile to the face of everyone who sees it.

*The African Queen*

Just north of Tavernier near MM93 on the gulfside of the highway is the **Florida Keys Wild Bird Rehabilitation Center** (daily 8am–6pm, tel: 852-4486). Down a gravel road hidden behind clumps of trees, the center is one of the most important bird sanctuaries in all of south Florida. Run by teacher Laura Quinn, it relies on volunteer veterinarians who take in injured and sick birds, nurse them back to health, and when they are fully recovered, set them free. Birds in residence include herons, vultures, falcons, anhingas, cormorants, pelicans, bobolinks, frigates, storks, ospreys, hawks, eagles and parrots. The center sells aviary supplies and books, and has a nature trail that snakes through a mangrove forest dotted with cactus plants and plum trees. It charges no admission fee, but donations are always welcome.

*Recuperating at the Wild Bird Center*

**19**

The town of **Tavernier** (65 miles/105km) was founded in the late 1800s, and at the turn of the century had the only post office between Miami and Key West. All that remains of the old town are a few turn-of-the-century buildings in the historic district, including a Methodist church, the post office, and several old wood frame houses with big hurricane shutters.

Generally a quiet and staid town with nothing but a few shopping centers and vacation houses, Tavernier is known throughout the Keys for being the location where dozens of 'Big Foot' sightings took place in the 1970s. Although never officially documented by scientists, many visiting fishermen and local residents said they spotted the mythical creature, part-man, part-beast, roaming through the mangrove swamps, leaving his (or her) huge and mysterious footprints.

# Tour 2

### ★★★ John Pennekamp Coral Reef State Park
*See map on pages 16–17*

*Boating in the park*

On the gulf side of the Overseas Highway, just north of Key Largo at MM102.5, **John Pennekamp Coral Reef State Park** (daily 8am–sunset, tel: 451-1621) is one of the greatest natural treasures of the Keys. The most visited state park in Florida, and the only underwater park in the continental United States, Pennekamp attracts over 2 million visitors a year and is considered one of the most popular diving spots in the world. The park is well-equipped to handle all these visitors, and several concessionaires on the grounds offer canoes, sailboats, scuba and snorkeling equipment for rent. It also has an excellent visitor center with information on marine exhibits, an aquarium, and tanks that allow visitors to touch the encased marine life. There are also several concession stands that serve a variety of foods and drinks.

Founded in 1960, Pennekamp was named after John Pennekamp, a Miami newspaper editor and conservation champion. The park was established to remedy the damage done during the 1930s and 1940s when local divers used to dynamite the reef in order to make it easier to gather shells and coral which they then sold to passing tourists. Today, the reef is rigorously protected with tough penalties for even the most minor assault – divers are forbidden to remove anything from the reef, or even to touch it. A mooring buoy system, allowing boats to tie up, protects the reef from being damaged by anchors.

*The Mangrove Walk*

Located about 3 miles (5km) offshore and covering almost 100 sq miles (260 sq km), Pennekamp's barrier reef is the third largest on earth. And despite decades of ecologically irresponsible tourism, industrial pollution, shoreline development and heavy boat traffic, it remains one of the most beautiful specimens of its kind in the world.

While it may appear to be nothing more than a giant coral rock, the reef is in fact a living, breathing organism, made up of millions of coral polyps that eat passing micro-organisms and extract calcium from seawater for additional sustenance. These small polyps constantly secrete a small amount of limestone which eventually takes different shapes, thus making for the wide varieties of coral – elkhorn, staghorn, brain, star, pillar, lettuce, and flower. The reef also provides nourishment and shelter for 400 species of marine life including fish, crabs, snails, sand dollars, starfish, sponges, lobsters and sea cucumbers. Left untouched, it has the capacity to grow 10 feet (3 meters) in overall size every 100 years.

In relatively shallow water, the reef is easy to explore, even for those who don't snorkel or scuba dive. **Glass-bottom boat trips** leave from the park's visitor center three times a day (9.30am, 12.30pm, 3pm; tel: 451-1621) and take non-swimmers for a two-and-a-half-hour tour over the reef with a view of pink and purple sea fans, mean-looking barracudas and sharks, slimy eels, human-size groupers, and electric blue angelfish, all underfoot.

*Glass-bottom boat*

The northernmost tip of the reef lies inside **Biscayne National Park** (headquarters at Convoy Point, east of Homestead, tel: 347-7275), a 181,000-acre (73,250-hectare) marine sanctuary. Biscayne is one of the largest national parks in the US, but has only a small area of shoreline and therefore receives relatively few visitors.

Although spread out over a large area, there are about 10 favorite spots of varied interest in Pennekamp Park that attract most of the attention. **Carysfort Reef**, named after a British frigate that ran aground before the Revolutionary War, is located close to a 100-ft (30-meter) lighthouse of the same name and marks the northernmost end of the most visited sites. The farthest from the commercial dive shops, Carysfort Reef is usually less crowded than many other reef sites. Its lighthouse, built in 1852, is the oldest functioning light of its kind in the world.

21

The mostly shallow waters of **White Banks Dry Rocks** are recommended to diving newcomers because they are almost always full of flashy and exotic fish. **French Reef** is popular because of its deep caves and canyons; and **Molasses**, the largest reef in the park, is strewn with sunken ships. Many of these barnacle-encrusted ships are a fascinating sight, but they have all been stripped bare of any treasures. There are also several modern-day wrecks that were deliberately sunk to create artificial reefs.

*Close-up view of exotic fish*

By far the most popular destination in Pennekamp Park is **Key Largo Dry Rocks**, site of the awe-inspiring **Christ of the Deep** statue. About 20 feet (6 meters) below the surface, the 9-foot (3-meter) high bronze statue is a replica of the Christ of the Abyss in the Mediterranean, off Genoa, Italy. Donated to the park by a wealthy Italian industrialist, the statue has outstretched arms and a mournful facial expression that looks upwards to the sky. It is dedicated to 'All who lived for the sea and who, in the name of the sea they so dearly loved, found their eternal peace.' Covered with a thin film of green algae, it is a sombre and mystifying sight.

*Christ of the Deep*

*Dolphin at the Theater of the Sea*

# Tour 3

**Tavernier – ★★ Islamorada – Long Key State Recreation Area** (25 miles/40km)

*Swimming with dolphins*

## Swimming with dolphins

One of the most popular things to do in the Keys is to swim with dolphins. The two attractions on the following pages that offer such adventures (Theater of the Sea and the Dolphin Research Center) are always booked months in advance. Since there are so many tourists and so few dolphins, the opportunities are limited and rather costly. But if the chance should arise, here are a few tips that might prove helpful.

The dolphins that you will see swimming are not the same dolphins that appear on local menus. The edible kind of 'dolphin' is a tropical game fish usually about 10 inches (25cm) long. The swimming kind of dolphin is a marine mammal that averages 7 feet (2 meters) in length.

The experience of swimming with such an animal can be intimidating. Although they are said to be 'gentle creatures,' and many people who have swum with them report an almost spiritual connection, dolphins in captivity have been known to be a little rough with people. They are reported to have bruised human swimmers on more than one occasion, and they have a strong, fishy odor.

Crossing over **Tavernier Creek**, the next cluster of islands includes **Plantation** and **Windley Keys**. Plantation was named for the many acres of pineapples and limes planted here at the turn of the century. At MM 84.5 on Windley Key is the ★★ **Theater of the Sea** (daily 9.30am–5.45pm, tel: 664-2431). The world's

*Well–trained seal*

second oldest marine park, Theater of the Sea has been attracting sea-starved tourists since 1946, and although it now has several more sophisticated competitors in the area, it is still an extremely popular family attraction. Housed in the pits of an old railroad quarry that dates back to the early 1900s, the 14-acre (5.5-hectare) park has two sea lions and 12 dolphins that put on action-packed shows, a 300-gallon (1,360-liter) 'living reef' aquarium, a touch tank, and alligator pond and a pool of hungry sharks. It also has a knowledgeable and helpful staff, and dozens of resident cats who do nothing but sleep and eat. With advance reservations, the Theater of the Sea offers tourists the chance to swim with its resident dolphins.

*Performing dolphins*

Less than a mile south, directly on the Overseas Highway, is the art deco-style **Hurricane Memorial** (MM82). It was in this area in 1935 that a powerful hurricane came ashore and this monument, with its depiction of huge waves and wind-bent trees, marks the site of the mass grave where 423 people were buried. Many of the victims of the storm were laborers working on the Overseas Highway, who were killed when a tidal wave overturned their evacuation train. In addition to the loss of lives, the 1935 storm with its 200mph (320kph) winds swept away just about every man-made object in the area at the time.

Near the Hurricane Memorial is the headquarters of the **Islamorada Chamber of Commerce** (tel: 664-4503), housed inside a red railroad caboose that serves as a reminder of the railroad that was once blown into the sea. Islamorada (pronounced eye-lah-mor-ah-dah) means purple island and was first so called by early Spanish explorers who, according to local legends, either named it after the purple blooms of bougainvillea plants, or in honor of the purple sea snails which clung to the shores. These days, the most important name Islamorada wants to be remembered by is the Sport-Fishing Capital of the World.

*Lumbering lobster*

Over the years, Islamorada's industries have included shipbuilding, farming, sponge-diving, wreck salvaging and turtling, but it wasn't until the town took the sport of fishing seriously that it really earned its place on the map. These days Islamorada has various tournaments that offer prizes for the biggest, smallest, weirdest and most fish caught. Islamorada is where former US President George Bush camped out to relax and toss a line in the water during his term in office. He did not, however, win any prizes.

*Purple bougainvillea*

Because of its closeness to the Gulf Stream, the water off Islamorada has always been teeming with big game fish and these days fishing-based tourism is its

main source of revenue. Dozens of bait-and-tackle shops, charter boat operators, and marinas line the highway. Those in the know follow the fishing seasons – sailfish from November to May, tarpon from March to July, bonefish from June to December, and blackfin tuna from November to April. Occasionally, Islamorada hosts shark tournaments that allow anglers to use shotguns as well as lines. Fishing is so ever-present in Islamorada that there is a museum dedicated to the sport. Located inside Bud 'n' Mary's Marina at MM80, the **Fishing Museum** (Monday to Saturday 10am–5pm) features a collection of antique tackle and poles, a video library, and photos of local catches.

Along with fishing, Islamorada is also well known as the place where the bars are always hopping, and its ★ **Holiday Isle Resort** (MM84.5, tel: 664-2321) is where much of the action takes place. A sprawling complex of hotels, restaurants, marinas, pools and shops, Holiday Isle is a haven for fun-seekers, especially on weekends when reggae blares from the outdoor bars. Its collection of ramshackle Bahamian-style shops called the **Bimini Boardwalk** is chock-full of unique clothing and crafts boutiques (the boardwalk gets its name from Bimini Island in the Bahamas).

*Holiday Isle Resort*

Three state parks in the Islamorada area offer some colorful history, and a peaceful refuge for those who easily tire of big fish stories. A ferry shuttles visitors from MM78.5 to **Lignumvitae Key State Botanical Site** (tel: 664-4815) where park rangers offer a two-hour guided tour of the 280-acre (113-hectare) island. Isolated in time and space when compared to the other Keys, Lignumvitae is one of the last remaining examples of what pristine vegetation in the Keys was once all about. All the plant life on the island is indigenous to Florida and includes over 130 species of trees, including the *lignum vitae*. A horticulturalist's dream, *lignum vitae* is the hardwood tree that native Indians once called the Tree of Life, and the Spanish thought had magical qualities. Full of resins that keep it from becoming brittle, *lignum vitae* wood is considered one of the very best for boat building and outfitting. Once prevalent in the Upper Keys, they have all but disappeared due to development. Other trees on the island are mahogany, mastic, banyan, hog plum, strangler fig, pigeon plum, poison wood and gumbo limbo.

*Key attractions*

The only sign of habitation on the island is the **Matheson House**, built in 1919 by the wealthy pioneering Matheson family who are remembered for the collection of Galapagos turtles they brought to the island. The four-bedroom coral rock house actually blew away during the 1935 hurricane, but was salvaged and pieced back together. The State of Florida acquired the island in 1972 and designated it a protected botanical site. Because of its fragile ecosystem, only 50 people are allowed on the island at one time. Also on Lignumvitae are cannons retrieved from the HMS *Winchester* which ran aground offshore in 1695, an ancient Caloosa Indian burial ground, and a 3,000-foot (915-meter) long coral rock wall. When or why the wall was built is a mystery which historians have not yet solved.

★ **Indian Key State Historic Site** can also be reached by a ferry that departs from MM78.5. A busy trading center that was known throughout the South for its incessant dancing and festivities during the early 1800s, Indian Key once had a population of over 400. Along with several shops and saloons, it had a grand hotel complete with a huge ballroom and bowling alley. The island was purchased in 1838 by botanist Henry Perrine, who planned to turn it into a commercial farm. In 1840 it was raided by Chief Chekika's Indian warriors during the Seminole War. Six people were killed, including Perrine, and all the buildings were burnt to the ground, ending habitation on the island. Most of Perrine's plants, however, survived, and today the 10-acre (4-hectare) uninhabited island is dotted with coffee, tea and sisal plants. Ranger guides offer visitors a historic walking tour down reconstructed village streets, and each spring the island hosts a festival in honor of its short but notorious history.

**25**

*Seminole brave*

*Birds of a feather*

To the south of these two state parks is **Lower Matecumbe Key**. This island got its name from the Spanish words *matar,* which means to kill, and *hombre,* which means man. During colonial times many shipwrecked sailors died on the island, others were taken captive by the Native Indians and turned into slaves.

The long narrow shoreline of **Long Key State Recreation Area** at MM67.5 (daily 8am–sunset, tel: 664-4815), about 15 miles (24km) south of Islamorada, is shaded by tall Australian pines and other tropical trees. On the Atlantic, the park has mangrove lagoons, an observation tower, nature trails, and wooden walkways snaking through dense foliage. Besides swimming and hiking, it is fun to rent a canoe and follow the marked waterway trails through the tidal lagoons.

Located 20 feet (6 meters) below the Atlantic about a mile south of Long Key is the **San Pedro Underwater Historic Preserve**. A 287-ton Spanish galleon sailing from Havana, the *San Pedro* sank here in 1733 when hurricane winds smashed it into the reef. The park has an underwater nature trail along with anchors, cannons and other nautical artifacts. No gates or gatekeepers, so you can explore any time you like.

**Long Key – Marathon – Looe Key** (30 miles/50km)
*See map on pages 28–9*

The **Long Key Bridge** (MM65.5) that connects Long Key with the small fishing village of **Conch Key** is technically the beginning of the Middle Keys. This long stretch of highway is one of the more dramatic in the Keys with wide horizon views on either side and a vast-ness of water so tempting that many drivers just have to pull over for a stop. The modern bridge lies adjacent to the old ★ **Long Key Viaduct**, Henry Flagler's most impressive expanse of railroad, and one of the most photographed spots in the Keys.

*Dolphin Research Center*

*Peacock stands aloof*

South of Conch Key is **Duck Key**, once the site of a salt-making factory and now a mostly residential island except for **Hawk's Cay Resort and Marina**. Although primarily a luxury resort, Hawk's Cay offers non-guests a chance to take a waterborne **ecology tour** led by a local naturalist who takes tourists to an uninhabited key and explains the many problems the local ecosystem is facing.

The 35-foot (10-meter) high jumping dolphin statue on the Gulf side of the road at MM59 is Mitzi, one-time star of television and movie *Flipper* fame. It marks the entrance to the Grassy Key ★★★ **Dolphin Research Center** (Wednesday to Sunday 9am–4pm, tel: 289-0002). The non-profit center, home to one of the world's largest populations of dolphins in captivity, is well respected throughout the US for its dolphin research and education programs and is located on the grounds of the former Flipper's Sea School. About a dozen resident dolphins live on the property, where they

*Looking for company*

are allowed to swim freely between fenced-in man-made lagoons and the wide open Gulf of Mexico. Many other sick, injured and stressed-out dolphins come from aquariums around the United States and are nursed back to health here. Dolphins, like humans, can develop ulcers and other stress-related illnesses when pushed to perform too hard.

The center also has specially designed programs for children with learning disabilities, cancer patient therapy, and a half-day program that teaches visitors about dolphin biology and human-dolphin communications. Dolphins, the center explains, have a language of clicks and whistles that enables them to communicate with each other and with humans. Its two-hour **Dolphin Encounter Program** enables tourists to swim beside, touch and play with the friendly, intelligent 7 ft (2m) long marine mammals in an open-air pool. As with most swim-with-the-dolphins attractions, reservations are required months in advance, but occasionally there are cancelations, so it is worth checking.

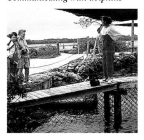

*Communicating with dolphins*

Continuing south on the Overseas Highway is a bridge that crosses over to **Vaca Key** and the northern end of **Marathon** (pop. 13,000). During the late 1700s Marathon was a tiny fishing village, but in 1818 a group of fishermen from New England settled on the island and transformed it into their own tropical paradise. During the early 1900s thousands of hard-working railroad men settled here, and because they regarded their long working days as a test of endurance, they named the town Marathon. The population of Marathon swells in winter months when snowbirds from up north come to escape the cold. Located in the center of the Florida Keys chain, the island is very developed, with several shopping centers, a hospital, and the **Marathon Airport**, the only commercial airport between Miami and Key West.

**27**

*Marathon Airport*

One of the things that draws so many people to Marathon is the fishing. Here, as in Islamorada, the highway is full of marinas, bait and tackle shops, and boat captains advertising their skills at angling. Unlike Islamorada, however, in Marathon and the rest of the Middle Keys, the sport of spear-fishing is legal, and spear-guns can be rented at most dive shops. Near MM50 is **Sombrero Docks**, one of the main departure points for the many deep-sea fishing boats that dock in Marathon. Other fishing centers are at **Key Colony Beach** and **Captain Hook's Marina**.

The ★★★ **Museum of the Florida Keys** and **Crane Point Hammock** at MM50 (Monday to Saturday 9am–4pm, Sunday noon–5pm, tel: 743-9100) is a 63-acre (25-hectare) nature sanctuary and educational

*Fishing at sunset*

*Florida Keys Museum exhibits*

center right in the middle of Marathon's commercial development. The museum's focus is on the natural history of the Florida Keys and features a re-created coral reef, shipwreck and American Indian artifacts, dug-out canoes, stuffed birds, and exhibits on local botany, geology and culture. Hidden in the rear of the main museum is the small but fun **Florida Keys Children's Museum** where kids can dress up in pirates' clothing and hop on a pretend ship, look through microscopes, explore an American Indian hut, walk alongside a Caribbean lagoon, and play with the hands-on exhibits.

All of this sits inside the Crane Point Hammock which is one of the area's most sensitive environmental and archaeological sites, containing the last known virgin palm hammock in North America. (A hammock is a patch of tropical trees, found in wetlands, usually an excellent habitat for wildife.) It contains about a dozen endangered plant and animal specimens and many exotic plants, flowers and birds. A quarter-mile (400m) educational trail in the hammock meanders past a late 1800s home, remnants of Bahamian buildings and pre-Colombian artifacts.

In an unpretentious little building at MM49, Marathon's **Cracked Conch Restaurant** (tel: 743-2233) is Florida Keys to the core and well worth a visit. Here, every imaginable way to cook conch is on the menu. From conch burgers to conch parmigiana and conch Benedict, the delicious marine snail is pounded into submission and then spiced to perfection. Once prevalent in the Keys, conchs were over-harvested years ago (*see Introduction, page 11*) and now almost all the conch meat used in local restaurants is imported from the Bahamas. It is still, however, a famous Keys food that deserves a taste.

Crossing the bridge

The **Hidden Harbor Turtle Hospital** (MM48.5, tel: 743-6509) is where Marathon motel owner and conservationist Richie Moretti, using proceeds from his business, has turned an old swimming pool into a tank for endangered sea turtles. Helped by volunteer veterinarians, he also takes in sick and injured pet turtles. The hospital has become highly regarded in the environmental community for its extensive research on a tumor-producing disease that is killing vast numbers of turtles all along the Atlantic coast.

The southern end of Marathon leads into a modern engineering marvel – the **Seven-Mile Bridge**. Completed in 1982 at a cost of $45 million, the bridge in fact is only 6.79 miles (10.9km) long, but nobody quibbles about a few yards. It is still the longest span in the Keys, and the longest segmental bridge in the world. And driving over the 40-foot (12-meter) high arch of concrete can be quite a challenge for those with a pho-

*A convalescent turtle*

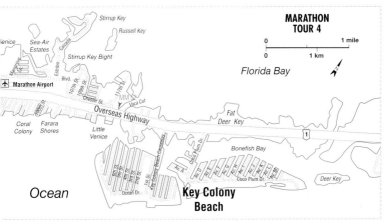

MARATHON
TOUR 4

bia about bridges or a fear of heights. Stopping on the bridge is not allowed. Each spring, runners gather in Marathon for the annual Seven-Mile Bridge Run.

Alongside the new structure is the original **Old Seven-Mile Bridge**, which was once called the Eighth Wonder of the World and is now listed on the National Register of Historic Places. Visitors can walk or bicycle along the old bridge, but no private vehicles are allowed. The two-lane span resting on 500 concrete piers was used for trains in its heyday, and was featured in the 1994 film *True Lies* starring Arnold Schwarzenegger. The old railings are worn and rickety, and trees now grow where trains used to run. The Florida Parks Department has wanted to turn the old bridge into a tourist attraction for years, but so far has been unable to find an entrepreneur willing to come up with an environmentally sound project, or the money to finance it.

*The Old Seven-Mile Bridge*

Off the end of a section of the Old Seven-Mile Bridge is **Pigeon Key**. A construction and maintenance facility for the railroad from 1908 to 1935, Pigeon Key is a 4-acre (1.5-hectare) island that has been designated as a National Historic District. In the early 1990s the local historical society restored seven early 1900s wooden buildings, and is working on a museum dedicated to the history of the railroad. In the meantime, visitors can view a 1930s black-and-white 'home movie' of a trip from Key West to Miami on the Florida East Coast Railway

*The quirky 7-Mile Grill*

A trip over the bridge wouldn't be complete without a stop first at the ★**7-Mile Grill** (MM47, tel: 743-4481). A quirky little restaurant that is quintessential Florida Keys, the 7-Mile Grill is an old favorite of locals who gather at the outdoor lunch-counter stools to gossip. A cluttered collection of old photos and mounted fish adorn the walls, and the shrimp bisque, crab salad, and chilled peanut butter pie are all absolutely delicious.

Past the Seven-Mile Bridge are **Little Duck**, **Missouri** and **Ohio Keys**. Near MM36.5 is ★★**Bahia Honda State Recreation Area** (daily 8am–sunset, tel: 872-2353) which has absolutely the best beach in the Keys. Spread out over 276 acres (112 hectares), the Atlantic coast park has broad stretches of sparkling white sand, a tropical lagoon, and walking trails that loop past patches of sea lavender, silver palm trees, spider lilies, morning glories and sea oats. The bird life in the park is especially active and sunbathers share the seashore with great white herons, giant ospreys and roseate spoonbills.

*Bahia Honda Beach*

A peculiar natural phenomenon of Bahia Honda

takes place each May during the full moon when tiny red palolo worms hatch from the rocks. Schools of tarpon fish gather to feast on the worms, creating a loud sucking sound that local anglers love to hear because it signals that the fishing will be great.

In Spanish, *bahia honda* means 'deep bay' and the waters just offshore at the southern end of the park are surprisingly deep for the Keys. Because of the depth, Bahia Honda is known for dangerous currents, and swimmers must be cautious. Concessionaires on the grounds offer cabanas, beach chairs, windsurf-boards, snorkeling equipment and kayaks for rent – there's a marked lagoon trail designed especially for the kayaks. There is also an air-conditioned restaurant and souvenir shop. Across the peninsula from the park is a dramatic view of a two-story section of the **Old Flagler Bridge**, the most difficult-to-build portion of the entire railroad.

It is from the Bahia Honda marina that boat trips to **Looe Key National Marine Sanctuary** can be arranged. Named after the *HMS Looe* (pronounced 'loo'), a British frigate ship that sank here in 1744, Looe Key is a 5-sq mile (13-sq km) protected coral reef that is every bit as breathtaking as John Pennekamp Coral Reef Park.

About 800 yards (730 meters) long and 200 yards (180 meters) wide, the reef is noted for the unusual grooves in its formation, which include complex clumps of elkhorn, staghorn and brain coral, and tall coral pillars that rise toward the surface like trees. There are also deep gullies and caves that plunge down 35 feet (10 meters), and thousands of exotic fish, rays, lobsters and octopuses. The remains of several wrecked ships, including the *HMS Looe*, lie within the sanctuary.

*Learning to fish*

**31**

*Bahia Honda marina*

# Tour 5

### Big Pine Key – Boca Chica Key (22 miles/35km)

Driving south from the **Bahia Honda Bridge**, the first large community is **Big Pine Key**, the beginning of what is considered the Lower Keys. The islands south of here tend to be much more heavily wooded and rugged than those in the Middle or Upper Keys. Geologically different from the other keys, most of the Lower Keys have a fossil coral base covered with a layer of limestone called oolite. Many are densely forested with sturdy pines and other tropical hardwood trees that are a favorite rooting spot for wild orchids.

*Big Pine Key: bands and buses*

The second largest island in the entire chain, Big Pine is 8 miles (13km) long and 2 miles (3km) wide. A curious mixture of commercial shopping areas and vast wildlife preserves, Big Pine has large pockets of development, but remains a quiet and relatively old-fashioned town where the battle between developers and environmentalists is constant. At MM31 is the **Lower Keys Chamber of Commerce** (tel: 872-2411), a good source of information on the area.

Several unique and endangered species still thrive in Big Pine and the Lower Keys. Among them are the cotton rat, the rice rat, the Vaca Key raccoon, the mud turtle and the Key Largo wood rat. But the most famous of these creatures is the **Key Deer**. The size of a small dog, Key Deer have been in the Keys since the islands were still attached to the mainland. Some scientists think that they originally crossed the low dry land that is now Florida Bay and, after years of isolation, underwent a slow genetic change that decreased their overall size.

DRIVE WITH CAUTION
YOU ARE ENTERING AN
ENDANGERED SPECIES
AREA PLEASE PROTECT
THE KEY DEER

DEER DEATHS
1996 104
THIS YEAR 3

*Protect the deer*

Considered a miniature subspecies of the mainland white-tailed deer, Key Deer in early Keys history were a source of food for local sailors and fishermen. But because of over-hunting and the destruction of their habitat, they became almost extinct, with only 50 left in the area by the end of the 1940s. In the late 1950s Big Pine Key established the ★ **National Key Deer Refuge** to insure their survival. By the 1970s their population had swollen to almost 800, but during the 1980s the deer herd dwindled again, largely due to development projects on the island. Today there are only about 300 of them – and each year about 50 Key Deer are killed in automobile accidents.

Information about the deer can be picked up at **Key Deer Refuge Headquarters** at the Big Pine Shopping Center, MM32 (Monday to Friday 8am–5pm, tel: 872-2239), but all it takes is a drive around Big Pine's

**Key Deer Boulevard**, or almost any desolate part of the island, to spot them. Delightfully tame and fragile creatures, Key Deer will eat out of your hand, but refuge rangers discourage tourists from feeding them and will in fact levy a fine on those who are caught. The best time to spot them is early morning and late afternoon, when the temperature drops slightly.

Key Deer can also be spotted on **No Name Key**, a sparsely populated island to the east of Big Pine Key, and on some of the other smaller islands in the Lower Keys. No Name Key made its way into the history books in 1962 when a group of Cuban refugees planning to invade their homeland took up residence on the island and began guerrilla training. One of the Cubans accidentally shot and killed a compatriot after he mistook him for a rabid raccoon.

Also on Key Deer Boulevard is **Blue Hole**, a 12-foot (3.5-meter) deep freshwater rock quarry lake – the only one of its kind in the Keys – with a substantial population of soft-shell turtles and a small family of large alligators. Blue Hole is on the **Pine Woods Nature Trail**. Nearby, signs point the way to the **Jack C. Watson Nature Trail**. A skilled hunter turned radical environmentalist, Jack C. Watson was an infamous Big Pine character in the 1970s who went so far as to sink the boats and burn the cars of poachers who killed deer. The hiking trail named after him meanders through a cool, dark hardwood forest full of Jamaican dogwood trees, bromeliads and giant spider webs. It's common here to spot mother deer feeding with their fawns.

The more commercial side of Big Pine is evident at the **Big Pine Village** on Overseas Highway at MM30.5. A slightly dilapidated open-air market, the village has a clustering of unique shops that sell everything from exotic parrots to tie-dyed clothing and fresh,

*Big Pine produce for sale*

33

*Reaching the heights*

*Shopping at Big Pine*

creamy fruit shakes. A short distance down the highway is the **Big Pine Flea Market**, a weekends-only outdoor market full of second-hand goods and hand-made crafts. The **Big Pine Coffee Shop** is a cozy little place where local fishing guides gather to compare notes on where the fish are running.

To the south of Big Pine are **Little**, **Middle** and **Big Torch Keys**, all named for the flammable torchwood trees that are prevalent on these islands. Torchwoods were often used as kindling by early homesteaders in the Keys because they will burn while still green. Some people say that their smoke has an hallucinogenic effect on humans.

To the east of Little Torch Key is **Little Palm Island** (tel: 872-2524), a private and pricey 5-acre (2-hectare) sand-covered island resort. Visitors are welcome on Little Palm and a free ferry departs from the Dolphin Marina at MM28.5 on the Overseas Highway every hour on the hour. With no cars, no television and only a few telephones, it is truly a great escape. A one-time fishing lodge that catered to US President Harry S. Truman, Little Palm has a private beach, Caribbean-style thatch-roof huts, and a lagoon-style pool that has had more than a few Key Deer come to visit. The resort's restaurant is considered one of the best in the Keys, featuring gourmet nouvelle cuisine masterpieces for lunch and dinner that are well worth the time and trouble of getting to the island.

**Ramrod**, **Summerland** and **Cudjoe Keys** are south of Little Torch. Summerland has a small private airstrip and lots of comfortable vacation homes. Cudjoe is noted for being the best spot to find fresh crayfish, and for its peculiar name, the derivation of which is uncertain. Some say it came from an early Key West homesteader named Cousin Joe. Others say it came from the island's joewood trees, while a few claim it came from the African slaves who were brought to Key West in the 1800s, and who frequently gave the name Cudjoe to a baby boy born on the first day of the week.

Floating above on most calm days is **Fat Albert**, a very sophisticated radar-equipped weather balloon that's moored to a missile tracking station on Cudjoe Key. Fat Albert, according to US government officials, keeps track of tropical storms that loom offshore. Those in the know, however, say that its real purpose is to monitor the smuggling of illegal drugs which is common in these waters, and to keep an eye on neighboring Cuba. An older version of Fat Albert broke free from its tethers a few years ago, and was shot down by the US Coast Guard.

Also near Cudjoe is the off-limits-to-visitors **Key**

*Big Pine Flea Market*

**Lois**, a scrappy little island approachable only by boat. Key Lois is owned by a medical research company, and is home to several hundred Rhesus monkeys. The island and its screeching, scratching inhabitants often come as a surprise to boaters who are unaware of their existence. Each evening, a caretaker arrives by boat bringing a supply of fresh water and several sacks of food for the monkeys.

A thriving community of sponge farmers when it was founded in the early 1900s, **Sugarloaf Key** is the next island in the chain. It is now full of plush suburban homes, and many of its residents commute to Key West for work. Sugarloaf is the name Bahamians gave to the pineapples that were once harvested on the island.

The **Sugarloaf Lodge** at MM17 is an old-fashioned luxury resort with a private airstrip, marina and tennis courts. A pond in front of its glass-enclosed restaurant is where Sugar, a very old and very tired dolphin, resides. At one time, Sugar had several companions, but local environmentalists caused such a commotion about them being used to entertain tourists that the lodge set some of them free and moved the rest to other marine sanctuaries. Sugarloaf small airport offers **sightseeing airplane rides** around the Lower Keys (tel: 745-2217).

*Taking it easy*

**Perky's Bat Tower** on Sugarloaf Key is one of the more notorious attractions in the Keys. Off Overseas Highway at MM17, this 35-foot (10-meter) tall pine curiosity was the brainchild of real estate developer Richter C. Perky who had the bright idea that by building a tower to attract bats – which supposedly eat mosquitoes – he would get rid of the menacing mosquito population in the area and then be able to build a luxury resort on the island. In 1929 he stocked his newly built tower with extremely smelly 'bat bait,' but the bats apparently did not find it attractive, and the mosquitoes remained a problem. Perky's innovative get-rich-quick plan failed and he went bankrupt.

*Serious fishing*

The last big island north of Key West is **Boca Chica Key** at MM10. During the 1930s Boca Chica was a casual, funky beach playground full of fishing camps and beer halls. During World War II the US military condemned the area and soon afterwards it was turned into a naval base for training pilots. A few old missile silos still stand, and fighter jets constantly land and take off. It was here, on the Boca Chica US Navy airstrip, that a Cuban pilot landed his Soviet MiG in 1991, much to the surprise of the air traffic controllers who had not spotted him on their radar. The pilot, a major in the Cuban Air Force, was granted political asylum by the US government.

*Bar in the Historic Seaport District*

## Tour 6

### ★★★ Old Town Key West
*See map on pages 40–1*

*Key West ticket seller*

Like the cherry on top of an ice-cream sundae, **Key West** (pop. 28,000) is the most treasured part of all Florida Keys vacations. Barely 4 miles (6km) long by 2 miles (3km) wide, it attracts over a million tourists a year, and packs more captivating attractions in one small place than any other area in Florida. An end-of-the-line, anything-goes kind of place, it is full of uninhibited charm and offbeat character.

### History
Discovered by Spanish explorers in the 16th century, Key West was originally called 'Cayo Hueso' (the Island of Bones) because of the human bones the Spaniards found scattered all over the island. Whether those bones belonged to the native Caloosa Indians or to drowned sailors, nobody really knows.

*Sponge man statuette*

For the most part, the island lay dormant until 1821 when Spain ceded Florida, including Key West, to the US. Soon after, the island received a small group of permanent British settlers (called Conchs) who came from the nearby Bahamas. In order to protect these settlers from marauding pirates, the US then established the first Navy Pirate Fleet in Key West. Throughout the early and mid-1800s, Key West grew, as developers and homesteaders came from all over the country.

By 1890 Key West was the richest city per capita in the United States, and the largest city in Florida. Sponge-diving, ship salvaging and cigar-making were its main industries. In 1912 the Florida East Coast

Railroad made its way to Key West, finally linking the island, and the rest of the Keys, to the Florida mainland. During the 1920s, after the US government had placed a prohibition on the manufacture, sale or consumption of liquor, Key West added rum-smuggling to its list of profitable businesses. From the 1930s to the 1950s, Key West established itself as a major tourist destination, luring American tourists to its exotic and tropical sites. Today, tourism is the mainstay of the local economy.

The entrance to the city is **Stock Island** at MM5. A bustling commercial district, Stock Island contains the **Tennessee Williams Fine Arts Center**, the **Key West Golf Course**, the massive garbage heap known locally as **Mount Trashmore**, and the **Oceanside Marina**, home-base for dozens of charter fishing boats.

The large 'Downtown' sign at the intersection of North Roosevelt Boulevard and Truman Avenue means the beginning of **Old Town**, the historic and main tourist area of Key West. In the northwest section of the island, with the parallel boundaries of Whitehead and White Streets, Old Town is a helter-skelter of grand Victorian homes, intimate guest houses, fancy restaurants, boisterous bars, art galleries, T-shirt shops, adult book stores, and eccentric street vendors.

*Classical Revival grandeur*

The ★ **Conch Train** (daily 9am–4pm, tel: 294-5161) at Mallory Square offers a 90-minute, 14-mile (22-km) tour around the city, pointing out 60 attractions on the way. The quaint-looking open-air tram rumbles through Key West as a narrator entertains the passengers with juicy stories and fascinating facts. With its canvas-canopied cars pulled by a mock railroad steam engine, the Conch Train has been operating in the city since 1958, and provides an ideal introduction to Key West. A similar tram tour is operated by **Old Town Trolley** (tel: 296-6688) which also departs from Mallory Square and several points on the island. The latter allows riders to get off to explore whenever they want and then hop back on when they are ready.

*Riding the Conch Train*

## Down Duval Street

The center of all the action in Old Town, and the busiest place in the city, is **Duval Street**. Although only 1 mile (1.5km) long, it has so many attractions that an entire day can be spent strolling from door to door.

**La-Te-Da** (1125 Duval Street), which is short for La Terraza de Marti, is one of the city's more unusual guest houses, and has a very good restaurant. A lush maze of tropical elegance, it was once the Key West home of exiled 19th-century Cuban poet and patriot José Martí. La-Te-Da, known for its flamboyant tea dances on Sun-

*Duval Street drag*

*Strand Theater*

*San Carlos Institute*

*Distinctive decoration*

day afternoons, caters to a gay clientele, but is the kind of place where anyone can feel comfortable.

**Ripley's Believe It Or Not Museum** at 527 Duval Street (daily 10am–11pm, tel: 293-9694) resembles all the other Ripley's 'odditoriums' around the world, but this one has a tropical/nautical focus. Among its collection are antique diving equipment, shrunken heads and a hurricane tunnel complete with blasts of gale force winds. Ripley's is housed in the former **Strand Theater**, an ornately beautiful art deco movie house, built in 1918.

Across the street from Ripley's is **Fast Buck Freddie's**, an only-in-Key-West kind of department store that specializes in masks for Halloween's Fantasy Fest, and bizarre gifts such as battery-operated alligators, animal-shaped furniture and pink flamingos in every size and shape.

Also on this block at 516 Duval Street is the **San Carlos Institute** (daily 9am–5pm, tel: 294-3887), a Cuban-American heritage center. It was founded in 1871 by immigrants who wanted to preserve their history and culture in Key West, and focuses on 19th- and 20th-century Cuban history. This is where Cuban patriot José Martí delivered his most passionate speeches in favor of his country's independence from Spain, and where Enrico Caruso, the best known operatic tenor of his time, once sang in its 400-seat opera house. The original structure was severely damaged by a fire in 1886, in which two-thirds of the city was destroyed, but rebuilt three years later. Threatened again by demolition in the early 1990s, it was saved by a $3 million State of Florida grant and now contains a research library, antiques, art, historic photos and films, and an impressive collection of Cuban memorabilia. A

detailed map for a self-guided **Cuban Heritage Trail**, which takes in 36 Key West sites with Cuban connections, can be picked up for free at the San Carlos Institute. Also on Duval Street is **Cuba! Cuba!**, a book, art, souvenir and cigar shop reminiscent of Havana in the 1950s.

Right next door to the San Carlos is the **Margaritaville Cafe**, a friendly joint where Cheeseburger-in-Paradise tops the menu and the owner, folk singer Jimmy Buffet, occasionally performs. Along with potent margaritas and greasy but good food, it has live music nightly and a gift shop that sells Jimmy Buffet tapes, books, T-shirts and souvenirs.

At 313 Duval Street is the **Hard Rock Cafe**, Key West's version of the international chain of shrines to rock-and-roll. In its 170-seat restaurant, the Hard Rock displays 300 pieces of music memorabilia, including a vest worn by Jimi Hendrix, a black dress worn by Madonna, Tom Petty's autographed top hat and, of course, an acoustic guitar owned by local hero Jimmy Buffet. Located inside a refurbished three-story Victorian-style mansion, the cafe attracts thousands of Hard Rock devotees who show up wearing those little Hard Rock Cafe pins that they've collected from around the world.

Not far from the Hard Rock Cafe at 322 Duval Street is the ★ **Wreckers Museum** (daily 10am–4pm, tel: 294-9502), a nine-room pine house that once belonged to local sea captain and wrecker Francis Watlington. Built in 1829 and considered the oldest house still standing in Key West, it contains a collection of wrecking artifacts, model ships, 18th-century antiques, and an intricately designed doll house complete with miniature Victorian furniture.

The oldest house of worship in Key West, established in 1838, is **St Paul's Episcopal Church** (its patron saint, St Paul, was a shipwreck victim). It stands tall and imposing amid the saloons on Duval Street, its white masonry facade embellished with stained-glass windows. St Paul's has massive bells that ring out over the town.

Although there are dozens to rave about, one saloon on Duval must be seen. **Sloppy Joe's**, said to be Hemingway's favorite watering hole, is a loud and boisterous joint. Old parachutes hang from the ceiling, peanut shells cover the floor, and posters and photos of Hemingway clutter the walls. Named for its founder, Captain Joe Russell, Sloppy Joe's was moved to this location in the late 1930s when Russell's landlord raised his rent from $3 to $4 per week. The real Sloppy Joe's, the one where Hemingway actually drank frozen

*Pondering the day's events*

**39**

*Hemingway Days at Sloppy Joe's*

*Mallory Square entertainer*

*The famous sunset*

daiquiris – was located a block away on Green Street.

At the northern end of Duval Street on the waterfront is ★★★ **Mallory Square**, a local institution with a hint of the old hippie days. In the early 1800s, salvaged goods were unloaded at the docks here and then sold at the auction blocks on the square. Since the late 1960s it has been the spot where thousands gather each evening for the sunset celebrations. As the bright red sun slips into the Gulf of Mexico, street performers entertain the crowds. Among the more eccentric regulars are a French lion tamer with house cats that jump through flaming hoops, a Hoodini-like bondage artist who slithers out of chains, a kilted bagpiper and a not-so-young lady who hawks chocolate chip cookies from her bicycle.

### Sites in Old Town

The **Key West Aquarium** (daily 10am–6pm, tel: 296-2051) at the foot of Whitehead Street is the oldest commercial tourist attraction in the Keys. Opened in 1935, it was the first open-air aquarium in the US. Its informative exhibits includes 40 tanks full of marine life, a touch tank, several sharks, and a turtle pool with a 400lb (180kg) green turtle named Porky. There is also a living coral reef that explains the ecological problems facing such a natural phenomenon.

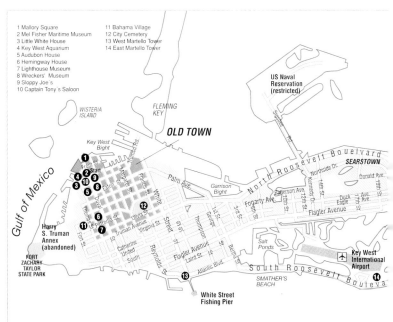

1 Mallory Square
2 Mel Fisher Maritime Museum
3 Little White House
4 Key West Aquarium
5 Audubon House
6 Hemingway House
7 Lighthouse Museum
8 Wreckers' Museum
9 Sloppy Joe's
10 Captain Tony's Saloon
11 Bahama Village
12 City Cemetery
13 West Martello Tower
14 East Martello Tower

Not far away is the ★ **Mel Fisher Maritime Heritage Society Museum** (daily 10am–5pm, tel: 294-2633). A gregarious old man, Mel Fisher astounded onlookers in the 1980s when, after a laborious 17-year search, he recovered the wrecks of Spanish galleons that sank in 1622 in the waters off the Keys. The *Atocha* and the *Santa Margarita* brought Fisher and his salvagers a booty worth about $4 billion. Much of this – gold bars, silver coins, cannons, gold chains and one brilliant 77-carat emerald – are on display in

*In the Mel Fisher Museum*

*Solid silver*

**41**

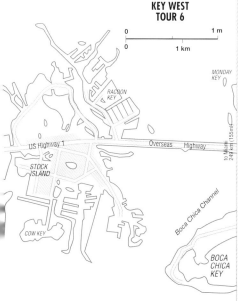

**KEY WEST
TOUR 6**

*Sword swallower
in Mallory Square*

his museum, along with an historic overview of the marine salvage industry in the Keys.

The very popular ★★ **Turtle Kraals** (tel: 294-2640) on the shrimp docks in the Land's End Village is both a waterfront restaurant and an historic landmark and turtle sanctuary. *Kraal* is an African word meaning holding pen. During the 1920s, turtles were brought to this spot from Nicaragua and the Caribbean to be held for shipment, or processed. Turtle Kraals was in business as a turtle cannery until the 1970s when turtle harvesting was declared illegal.

Today, Turtle Kraals has the most extensive exhibit on turtles in the world, including a pair of 20-year-old hawksbill turtles that are the sole survivors of Key West's turtle farming days, and several loggerhead turtles weighing up to 400 pounds (180kg). It also has a grim collection of machines once used to chop turtle meat into tiny pieces suitable for use in green turtle soup. The green turtle, a protected saltwater reptile now on the endangered species list, is no longer harvested for food.

*Audubon House*

*Tropical flower*

The **Little White House Museum** (daily 9am–5pm, tel: 294-9911) in the **Truman Annex** on Front Street is a former naval storehouse, built in 1890. Most of the military buildings have been turned into condominiums but one, the Little White House, remains as it was during the 1940s when President Harry S. Truman used it as a winter retreat. Truman often strolled around the neighborhood here talking to locals. Artifacts and antiques from his term in office are on display.

The **Audubon House and Garden** (daily 9.30am–5pm, tel: 294-2116) is a magnificent three-story mansion, set in lush grounds, which was built in the 1840s to commemorate American ornithologist James John Audubon's 1832 visit to Key West. Audubon spent a few weeks walking through Key West mangroves while researching his book *Birds of America*. Although of course Audubon never visited this house, it has a folio of his original engravings produced between 1826 and 1838, along with many 18th- and 19th-century antiques from around the world. You can also take a self-guided walking tour through the tropical garden.

It's easy to see why the most visited site in Key West is the ★★★ **Hemingway House** at 907 Whitehead Street (daily 9am–5pm, tel: 294-1575). This two-story Spanish colonial mansion was the first house in Key West to have running water, a pool, a fireplace and a basement. It was here in the 1930s that Ernest Hemingway wrote many of his finest works and today it is a museum dedicated to the author. He lived here with his second wife Pauline, their two sons and several ser-

*The Hemingway House*

vants, having purchased the house for $8,000 with money from his wife's wealthy uncle. The porcelain urinal, now a birdbath, that sits near the pool was dragged back to the house by a drunken Hemingway from the rest-room of a local saloon. The pool was built by Mrs Hemingway in the 1930s as a surprise for her husband, and much of the dense foliage surrounding the home was planted by the nature-loving writer himself.

Shortly after Hemingway died in 1961, a local woman named Bernice Dickson bought the house from his estate and transformed it into a literary shrine filled with antiques, Venetian glass, old books, hunting trophies, writing tools and a ceramic cat given to the author by Pablo Picasso. The museum staff offer well-informed tours with lots of colorful Hemingwayesque tales. The house is still home to about 50 cats, many of which are said to be descendants of Hemingway's original collection of six-toed felines.

*Contented cats*

If a quick stop at Hemingway's house is not enough, local historians offer a one-hour **Writers' Walk** tour which goes past the homes of prominent authors who have lived in the city. On Saturday mornings the tour departs from 410 Caroline Street, and on Sunday mornings it leaves from the Hemingway House.

Just a few houses down the block from the Hemingway Museum is the **Lighthouse Museum** (daily 9.30am–5pm, tel: 294-0012). The museum, located inside an 1887 clapboard house, with an adjacent 92-foot (28-meter) lighthouse, contains artifacts from the city's maritime history, charts, photographs, military uniforms and model ships. The lighthouse and its observation deck, which are listed on the National Register of Historic Places, offer a panoramic view of the city and its waterfront.

*Hemingway's study*

Located at the foot of Whitehead Street, on the wa-

*Southernmost Point*

ter's edge, is the ★ **Southernmost Point**. Though it's nothing more than a massive concrete buoy with red and yellow stripes around it, this is one of the most photographed sights in Key West. In fact, the claim is technically incorrect (the real southernmost point in the continental US is located at the nearby naval base which is off-limits to the public) but this is the southernmost point available to tourists. The buoy was installed here in 1983 by city officials who got tired of replacing the Southernmost Point signs that were constantly being stolen by drunken souvenir hunters.

*Captain Tony's Saloon*

Mingling with inebriated tourists and locals is part of the attraction of Key West, and one of the best spots to do this is at ★★ **Captain Tony's Saloon** on Green Street. This is the original site of the old Sloppy Joe's, and the two saloons have a long-standing rivalry. The oldest bar in the city, Captain Tony's is dark, damp and a bit peculiar: it once served as the Key West morgue. For decades it was owned by Tony Tarracino, a former bootlegger, gambler, gun-runner, mercenary and one-time mayor of Key West. Along with wickedly strong drinks, it features live rhythm-and-blues and country music.

While not nearly as grand as the Hemingway House, the **Tennessee Williams House** at 1431 Duncan Street does attract a few of the writer's curious fans. This modest white house behind a picket fence is where the Pulitzer Prize-winning playwright lived and worked for about 30 years. It is not open to the public, as it was sold to the current owners with the stipulation that it should never be turned into a tourist attraction.

For a glimpse and a sniff of the history of the cigar in Key West, **Key West Cigar Factory** and the **Caribbean Cigar Factory**, both on the narrow little street known as Pirate's Alley, are the places to go. The original Key West Cigar Factory dates back to the mid-1800s, and was larger than this tiny shop. But here, and

*Hand–rolled cigars*

next door at the up-scale Caribbean Factory, you can still see cigars rolled by hand in the old-fashioned way.

The best book- and newsstand in Key West is **Valladares Newsstand**. Along with international newspapers and magazines, it has a helpful selection of books about the Keys.

**Key West Aloe** on Front Street is the headquarters and factory of this chain. Founded in 1971, it is a local institution that now produces over 300 aloe-based skin care products. The factory offers a tour that explains how the plants are grown, processed and then blended.

The **Donkey Milk House** at 613 Eaton Street, now filled with antiques and artifacts, with Spanish tiled floors, got its name from the donkey milk carts that

*Key West Aloe*

gathered in front during the late 1800s. Built in 1866 by a prominent local businessman, the Classic Revival structure was preserved from the fire of 1886 when the owner dynamited part of the street in order to save the house and others nearby. In fact, a portion of this house was moved here from another location across town.

## Bahama Village

*Bahama Village house*

Bordered by Angela, Petronia and Olivia Streets, the historic neighborhood known as **Bahama Village** is exactly that. During the 18th century, hundreds of Bahamian settlers and West Indian slaves were brought to Key West to help build the city. Their knowledge of tropical plants and hurricane-resistant architecture proved valuable to Key West, and many of their original homes still stand.

Although it looks run down and is not one of the more prosperous areas of the city, Bahama Village is full of brightly painted small wooden houses with tin roofs that look very West Indian. Descendants of these early Bahamians still live here and it's easy to find some spicy conch fritters being sold on the street. A few galleries specializing in Haitian and Caribbean arts and crafts line the streets.

**45**

One of the worth-tracking-down sites here is ★ **Blue Heaven** (Wednesday to Sunday 7.30am–3pm and 6–10pm) on the corner of Thomas and Petronia Streets. This Greek Revival clapboard house is now a popular restaurant with healthy foods served under enormous tropical trees. Years ago, it served as a bordello, a boxing ring and a cock-fighting arena. A few resident roosters still roam the perimeter, the only reminders of its raucous past. It's a good place for families and there is sometimes live music in the evening.

*Bahama Village rush hour*

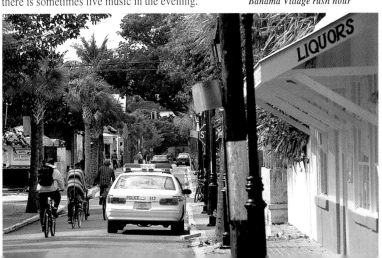

*Cat on look-out duty*

# Tour 7

## Around Key West: Forts and Beaches

On the southeast side of the island, facing the Atlantic Ocean, Key West has three historic fortresses built in the mid-1800s to protect against enemy attack. Now listed on the National Register of Historic Places, the solid brick **East Martello Tower** on South Roosevelt Boulevard was never completed, as advances in arms technology rendered the old fort obsolete. It was created to fend off coastal attacks during the Civil War, its unusual cylindrical shape resembling a medieval castle. Its Corsican design includes a tower with vaulted ceilings and a spiral staircase.

*East Martello Tower Museum*

The top of the tower provides an expansive view of the island and the Atlantic, exactly what it was meant to do. Inside, a small area contains a museum that houses artifacts and military uniforms from the *US Maine*, a battleship that was blown up in Havana Harbor during the Spanish-American War.

The primary reason to visit East Martello is the ★ **East Martello Historical Museum and Art Gallery** (daily 9.30am–5pm, tel: 296-3913). The museum, managed by the Key West Art and Historical Society, is overflowing with local artifacts. There are dramatic exhibits on Native Indians, the Overseas Highway, the Flagler Railroad, the cigar and sponging industries, and a very valuable collection on Cuban Key West history. Inside the brick arches and cracking walls of the 13 vaulted rooms, some of the more unusual artifacts include travel posters and airline tickets from the early 1950s when Key West was the departure point for US tourists going to Cuba, a horse-drawn hearse that was used to transport the bodies of soldiers killed during the Spanish-American War, a collection of movie memorabilia produced in the vicinity, and a flimsy bamboo raft, with a tobacco sack for a sail, which was used by Cuban refugees who sailed to Key West.

The museum also has a Key West Writers' Room with glass cases containing books written by the many celebrated authors who have lived on the island *(see Literature and Lore, page 58)*.

*Bell on display*

The fort's art gallery features permanent and changing exhibits. The primitive wood carvings of local artist Mario Sanchez, and the weird 'junk art' of Key Largo's Stanley Papio are always on display. A junk dealer by trade, Papio utilized old bed frames, car parts, bathroom fixtures and kitchen appliances. He was arrested many times by the local authorities for having too much junk in his front yard, but after his death in 1982 his work came to be regarded as art and admired for its statements about contemporary society.

About 2 miles (3km) west of the East Martello Tower is its sister, the **West Martello Tower**. It was built in 1861 and used as a lookout post during the Spanish-American War. More weather-beaten and tarnished and considerably less impressive than the East Tower, West Martello has been the victim of thieves and vandals who have stolen or damaged its brickwork. It was also used as a target for gunnery practice, which accounts for its pock-marked facade. Inside the tower is the headquarters of the **Key West Garden Club** (Wednesday to Sunday 10–11.30am and 1.00–3.30pm, tel: 294-3210), a group of local horticulturalists who host several orchid shows and plant sales throughout the year.

**47**

The third fort in Key West is at **Fort Zachary Taylor State Park** (daily 8am–sunset, tel: 292 6713), on the west side of the island. Named for the twelfth president of the United States, the Fort Taylor ruin is a major Civil War archaeological treasure. It was built between 1854 and 1866, tough years of hard labor, yellow fever epidemics and hurricanes. During the Civil War it served as home base for a blockade of ships, and is one of the reasons why Key West was the only southern US city to remain in Union hands.

*Fort Zachary Taylor and its cannons*

Decades later it earned the title Fort Forgotten, buried under tons of sand. But in 1968 a group of local historians began shoveling away the sand and in the next decade not only uncovered the trapezoid-shaped red brick fort, but also excavated thousands of cannonballs, bullets and cannons. A few years later an armament museum was created to house the finds. Fort Taylor contains the largest number of Civil War artifacts in the United States.

*Shoals of fish*

*Higgs Beach*

*Welcome to the beach*

Adjacent to the fort is a 50-acre (20-hectare) state park with plenty of picnic tables and barbecue grills, and the best beach in Key West. Less crowded than most of the city's other beaches, and frequented more by locals than tourists, this one is not just good for sunning and swimming, but also for snorkeling. An artificial reef teems with fish just yards from the beach. Bring a picnic, because the only concession stand has little to offer.

Aside from Fort Zachary Taylor State Park, the beaches in Key West are not nearly as nice as those in other parts of the Keys. Most Key West's are made from sand shipped in from elsewhere in Florida or the Bahamas, and are dotted with clumps of seaweed and small coral rocks.

The longest and narrowest strip of sand in Key West is **Smathers Beach**, on South Roosevelt Boulevard just south of the Key West International Airport. Smathers is a spot favored by avid sun-worshippers. It is also one of the best areas in the city for windsurfing, parasailing, kite-flying and overall beachside fun. Dozens of rental equipment concession stands line the road, as do hot food and cold drink vendors.

Across the highway is the **Thomas Riggs Wildlife Refuge**, containing disused salt ponds. Not very picturesque but a good place to see wading birds feeding among the thick grasses.

**Higgs Beach**, near the West Martello Tower on Atlantic Boulevard, between White and Reynolds Streets, is popular with families. Along with safe and shallow waters, it has an inviting fishing pier, a playground, a bathhouse and picnic tables. About five blocks away, at the end of Vernon Street, there is a small beach area where topless bathing is allowed.

## Key West City Cemetery

Visiting cemeteries might not be everybody's idea of a good time, but a stroll through the **Key West City Cemetery** (daily, sunrise–sunset) offers an amusing glimpse into the more quirky side of the city, along with colorful snippets of local history and humor, and one truly macabre testimony to unrequited love. In the middle of a residential Old Town neighborhood, the cemetery is open during daylight hours and its main entrance is on Margaret Street. Guided tours are available on weekends at 10am and 4pm (tel: 296-3913).

*The City Cemetery*

The cemetery was offficially opened in 1847, after a devastating hurricane of 1846 had destroyed the island's early burial grounds, but many of the graves here date back to the early 1800s. The Key West City Cemetery, initially rather small, grew with time to sprawl over 21 acres (8 hectares) and now contains more than 35,000 burial sites. Because it is so jam-packed, caretakers occasionally recycle old tombs in order to make room for new ones. A few frangipani trees and park benches provide respite from the constant heat and blindingly white sun, and hawks, buzzards and gulls often swoop down between the tombs.

**49**

Due to a high water table and a coral rock foundation, all the tombs are in above-ground vaults. Many are decorated with glass-encased photographs of the occupant. Some are adorned with ordinary plastic flower arrangements; others are festooned with feathers, candles, ornaments and other paraphernalia used in voodoo and Santeria ceremonies which are practiced by some local residents. While there are no real celebrities buried here, there are lots of people who continue to be as idiosyncratic in death as they were in life.

*'My Best Buddy'*

Many of the tombs have nothing but endearing nicknames inscribed in stone – Shorty, Mamie, Bunny, The Taylor. A few have playful epitaphs such as 'I Told You I Was Sick,' 'A Devoted Fan Of Singer Julio Iglesias,' 'Call Me For Dinner' and 'The Buck Stops Here.' Beside Earle Saunders Johnson's grave is a life-size sculpture of Saunders, complete with his own boots. Family pets – iguanas, dogs, snakes, birds and cats – have been included, too. Standing in front of one memorial is a statue of Elfina, a much-loved pet Key Deer. The Otto family plot contains the remains of three cherished Yorkshire terriers.

Several sailors who lost their lives aboard the *USS Main* when it exploded in Havana Harbor in 1898 are buried in a plot marked by a statue of a sailor, erected

*USS Main memorial*

*Peaceful resting place*

in their honor. Another monument is dedicated to **Los Martires de Cuba** in honor of Cuban revolutionaries who lost their lives fighting in the Spanish-American War. Sloppy Joe Russell, owner of the famous Sloppy Joe's bar on Duval Street and inspiration for Hemingway's novel *To Have and Have Not*, is buried here, as is Abe Sawyer, a local midget who, in accordance with his final wish, was laid to rest inside a full-size coffin. The largest tomb in the cemetery belongs to William Curry, Florida's first millionaire and original owner of the city's Curry Mansion.

Although unmarked, the most bizarre site in the cemetery is the **grave of Elena Hoyos Mesa**. A dazzling young Cuban beauty, Elena died of tuberculosis in 1931. A deranged medical technician named Karl von Cosel was madly in love with her, and following her death visited her grave every day. Totally obssessed with his lost love, a few years later he dug up her body, carried it home, preserved it in wax, inserted glass eyes, dressed it in a silk gown and, allegedly, made love to it every night.

For seven years this necrophilous love affair continued, until the authorities discovered Elena's mummified remains. Fascinated by the horror and pathos of the story, thousands of Key West residents attended a second public wake for Elena. Soon after, she was returned to a grave and von Cosel was arrested. The judge presiding over the case decided that the statute of limitations on grave-robbing had expired, and charges against von Cosel were dropped. When he died in 1952, he took a life-size replica of Elena to his grave with him. In the early 1990s, local writer Ben Harrison published *Undying Love*, a gripping and truthful account of this stranger-than-fiction tale.

*Well–tended tomb*

# Excursion

★ **Fort Jefferson – Dry Tortugas National Park** (Key West to Fort Jefferson: 70 miles /112km by air or sea)

A few specks of land sitting in the Gulf of Mexico about 70 miles (112km) west of Key West, **Dry Tortugas National Park** is a rugged, barren site surrounded by dramatically blue and crystal clear waters. The Dry Tortugas are geographically a part of the Florida Keys island chain, but they have never been linked by road or rail. The Spanish explorer Juan Ponce de León first called these tiny islands the Tortugas because of the many sea turtles he spotted sunning on their shores – *tortuga* is Spanish for turtle. A few years later passing sailors added the word Dry because of the lack of fresh water on the islands.

The Tortugas consist of seven keys – Bush, East, Garden, Hospital, Loggerhead, Long and Middle Keys – but they are all tiny. Loggerhead is the largest, and that is only 25 acres (10 hectares).

Covering almost all the 16 acres (6 hectares) of **Garden Key**, the massive, hexagonal **Fort Jefferson** appears peaceful today, but at one time was considered the most dreaded prison in the whole of the United States, and many people say that an eerie sense of gloom and loneliness still hangs in the air.

**51**

*Isolated Fort Jefferson*

After Florida became part of the United States in 1821, military officials recognized the strategic importance of the Dry Tortugas, and realized that the nation which occupied them would control navigation in the Gulf. So it was decided to build Fort Jefferson. Utilizing hundreds of slave laborers, dozens of skilled craftsmen, and millions of red bricks, construction of the hexagonal fortress began in 1846 and continued for 30 years. Although technically never completed, it is the largest coastal fortification ever built in the United States and is often called the Gibraltar of the Gulf of Mexico.

*Massive fortifications*

Its 8-foot (2.5-meter) thick walls stand 50 feet (15 meters) tall and feature sweeping stone archways and well-designed ramparts. The three gun tiers were designed to accommodate 450 guns. Except for a few cracks in the foundation, it appears as it did in the late 1800s – solid and sound, especially to the eye of the average visitor who is usually amazed at its impenetrable magnitude.

Fort Jefferson, originally intended to protect the US trading ships that frequented the area, was used during the American Civil War as a military outpost to hold captured deserters as prisoners. Federal troops were stationed there in 1861, but the fort was never fired upon, nor called upon to fire on a passing ship.

Largely ignored by the war-time Confederate troops, Fort Jefferson's most important claim to fame took place after the Civil War when in 1865 four men connected with the assassination of President Abraham Lincoln were imprisoned there. One of these men, Dr Samuel Mudd, the physician who had set the broken leg of Lincoln's assassin, John Wilkes Booth, was eventually pardoned for good behavior after he treated hundreds of prisoners who became ill during a yellow fever epidemic in 1867. During those years, about 800 prisoners were locked inside the fort's dark, depressing dungeon and life for them was truly tortuous – the temperature was scorchingly hot, the mosquitoes ravenous, the hurricane winds brutal, the lack of water a constant problem, and the wardens infamous for their cruelty.

*A national monument*

No longer of any strategic value, the fort was abandoned by the US Army in 1874. In 1935 President Franklin D. Roosevelt declared it a national monument, and later, in 1992, it was designated a national park and wildlife sanctuary. Today it serves as the serene and safe nesting ground for numerous species of birds, and a stopping-off place for many others, as it is in the migration flight path. Sooty terns, frigates, brown pelicans and cormorants can all be seen here in great numbers. Some of them fly great distances to lay their eggs on Bush Key, in the dry, scrubby vegetation they prefer. Because of this influx, a great many of the 30,000 tourists who visit Garden Key and its sister islands each year, especially during March, April and May, are avid bird watchers.

*Visiting pelican*

Unless you have access to a private boat, there are only two ways to get to Fort Jefferson. The quickest is by taking a 30-minute commercial flight from Key West on either **Key West Seaplane Service** (5603 College Road, Key West, tel: 294-6978) or **Chalks Airlines** (1 Duval Street, Key West, tel: 292-3637). Flights leave Key West early in the morning (Key West Seaplanes sometimes have a second flight around noon, but check details in advance as flight times may change) and return in the late afternoon. The planes are small and soon get filled up, so advance reservations are required, but the view from their windows as they approach the fort is breathtaking.

If you prefer a more leisurely trip, **Yankee Fleet** boats (PO Box 5903, West Key, tel: 294-7009) leave the Land's End Marina at 7.30am on Monday, Wednesday and Saturday, returning at about 7pm. It's a lovely cruise, and breakfast is served on board, but the jour-

*The fort's imposing entrance*

ney takes three hours each way, which does not leave you much time at Fort Jefferson.

Once they are on dry land, visitors can have a look around the small museum, and view an informative slide show, before setting off to explore this remote area. There is plenty to do: you can go on a self-guided walking tour, stroll along the pristine beach, spread out a picnic, or snorkel in the shallow, amazingly clear waters. Offshore there is a cluster of seven coral reefs, plenty of colorful marine life, and four species of endangered turtles: the green turtle, the hawksbill, the leatherback and the Atlantic. Not far from the shoreline several sunken ships lie below the surface.

Fishing is a popular sport in the Dry Tortugas all the year round, although you must remember to get a fishing license in advance (*see Active Vacations section on page 68*).

There are public toilets on the island and snorkeling equipment is available for rent, but Fort Jefferson is definitely a no-frills excursion – there are no restaurants or food vendors. Remember to to bring along a packed lunch, an adequate supply of drinking water, and anything else you might need during the day, including plenty of sun-block and a hat to protect you from the sun's rays. And since there are no garbage containers on the island, all your trash must be carried back to Key West when you leave.

If one day is just not enough, and you feel like staying overnight, camping is allowed, but on Garden Key only. Toilets, barbecue grills and picnic tables are provided and the campsites are free, but they cannot be booked in advance, so you must stake your claim when you first arrive in the morning, or you may be disappointed. It is pretty basic, but it's a beautiful place to wake up in the morning.

*Marine life*

*Bottles for divers*

# Architecture – Tropical Charm

All along the Florida Keys chain, most of the architecture is nondescript and modern; new stilt houses alongside coral rock cottages and flamingo-pink resorts. The Upper and Middle Keys were all but barren until the railroad came to town in the early 1900s. But in Key West there exists a definite vernacular style.

During its heyday – it was the richest city per capita in the US in 1890 Key West had over 650 houses. The islanders gave their name, Conch, to the style of architecture they created. Most of the people who built these houses were shipbuilders who copied various styles from the many ports they had visited – New Orleans, the Bahamas, and those on the coast of New England – and incorporated them in their Key West creations. Many of these structures still stand today and their wide porches and verandahs, overhanging eaves, kitchens housed in separate buildings, louvered shutters, filigree trellises, nautical cedar beams and rooftop widows' walks are all symbols of the Key West architectural style.

*A typical verandah*

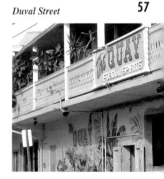
*Duval Street*

**57**

The more Key West prospered, the more these homes took on innovative designs, with elaborate gables, gingerbread fretwork and broad bay windows added in later years. This combination of whimsical and eccentric styles is definitive of what locals now call Classical Revival. Intentionally designed to protect against heat, light and tropical storms, many of these historic Key West houses withstand hurricanes much better than their more modern concrete counterparts.

In the mid-1970s, a massive survey of Key West's early architecture was conducted, and over 3,000 historic structures were placed on the National Register of Historic Places. Key West now holds the largest number of architectural or historical sites in one area in Florida. Buildings in the Old Town are protected by the strict regulations of the Historic Architecture Review Commission, which places restrictions even on such things as the color of exterior paint allowed.

Until about 20 years ago, visitors could only admire these houses from the street but today many of them have become guest houses or small inns. There are several well-researched walking tours of the town, and historic architecture maps available from the chamber of commerce. The best areas to explore are Eaton Street, from William to Duval; William Street, between Caroline and Southard; Elizabeth Street, from Angela to Flemming, and the area known as Bahama Village which has the largest number of un-gentrified Conch houses left in the city (*see Tour 6, page 45*).

*Early architecture*

## Literature and Lore

The Florida Keys are full of romantic stories, and the people who write them. Ever since Ernest Hemingway made Key West his winter home in the 1930s, the islands have been a Mecca for literary greats, as well as literary not-so-greats. Hemingway helped place the obscure Florida Keys on the world map, and made it one of the most popular literary retreats in the whole of the United States. It was in Key West that Hemingway first met writer Martha Gellhorn, whom he later married. And it was in Key West that he spent the most productive years of his life, writing *A Farewell to Arms*, *Death in the Afternoon*, and *For Whom the Bell Tolls*. The big yellow house where he lived is now one of the most visited tourist attractions in the city.

*The Hemingway House*

Following in Hemingway's path a flock of noted writers descended upon the Keys. Among them were John Malcolm Brinnin, John Hersey, Alison Lurie, James Kirkwood, James Merrill, Richard Wilbur, John Dos Passos, Elizabeth Bishop, Robert Frost and Tennessee Williams.

Williams first landed in Key West in 1941 and then spent most of his winters on the island until his death in 1983. Several of his best plays were written here, including *Night of the Iguana* and *The Rose Tattoo*, which was later filmed in the city. With Hemingway then living in Cuba, Williams was the reigning literary king of the Keys during the 1950s and 1960s, a time when he often hosted outrageous parties for his friend, the author Truman Capote.

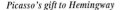

*Home to Hemingway cats*

Williams, along with his entourage of gay companions and friends, was instrumental in attracting hundreds of gay writers, artists and musicians to Key West during the late 1950s and 1960s. Many of them bought homes and established guest houses and galleries in Key West and the Lower Keys, and later contributed to the overall gentrification and revitalization of the area during the 1980s.

*Picasso's gift to Hemingway*

In more recent years a younger, more hip group – Joy Williams, Thomas Sanchez, Annie Dillard, Thomas McGuane, Laurence Shames, Philip Caputo and folk singer-cum-novelist Jimmy Buffet have made Key West their writing habitat. All in all, nine of them have been awarded the Pulitzer Prize, and Hemingway, of course, won the Nobel Prize in 1954.

In addition to the fact that so many literary giants came to this tiny tropical place, Key West has a certain live-and-let-live atmosphere which is always attractive to artistic people, and writers continue to stream into Key West and the surrounding Keys.

# Fantasy Fest

Perhaps the most significant cultural aspect of the Keys, and of Key West in particular, is its flamboyant penchant for fantasy and nonconformity. Living for the moment and acting out one's dreams – be they writing murder mysteries, painting seascapes, drinking with drug smugglers or dressing up in sequins and feathers – is the cornerstone of life for many who have chosen to live in the Keys.

This turn-your-fantasy-into-reality mentality is demonstrated most fervently at Fantasy Fest, the annual Halloween bash in Key West. Since its inception in 1979, Fantasy Fest has grown from a playful costume street party to one of the largest and most outrageous adult-rated extravaganzas in the United States. With a predominantly gay following, the week-long festival is cheerfully uninhibited and features exotic masked marches, a parade of floats, drag queen contests, elaborate grand balls, tea dances and even pet masquerades.

*Key West goes wild*

The event, which is often called Florida's Mardi Gras, has been graced with some of the biggest names in US entertainment – Herbie Mann, Jimmy Buffet, Chaka Khan, Grace Jones. But it has also been criticized by local authorities for going too far – naked and half-dressed revelers, pornographic costumes and general lewd and vulgar behavior have upset some people, and a few years ago there was talk of banning it altogether. But a few compromises were made on both sides, and now most people seem to take the Fantasy Fest in their stride. It has become a local tradition, one that personifies the penchant for fantasy and fun which is a Key West characteristic.

59

*What big teeth you have…*

*Renaissance Fair*

*Knights of old*

# Events Calendar

**Second weekend in January**: **Key West Literary Festival** – seminars, workshops, readings and literary walking tours. From mysteries to biographies, poetry and screenwriting, topics change each year but always attract distinguished literary figures as well as numerous aspiring writers.

**Mid-January: Florida Keys Renaissance Fair** – Marathon puts on a 16th-century-style fair with knights on horseback, jugglers, jesters, mimes and wandering minstrels.

**Mid-January: Railroad Days** – Key Largo pays tribute to the historic East Coast Railroad.

**January–March: Old Island Days** – a three-month celebration of local history featuring house and garden tours, concerts, plays, arts and crafts, flower shows and conch-blowing contests.

*Renaissance chic*

**End of February: Islamorada Sport-Fishing Festival and Blessing of the Fleet** – fishing competitions with big prizes and boat races.

**End of February: Civil War Days** – Fort Zachary Taylor Park in Key West hosts a mock Civil War invasion and occupation of the fort by Union soldiers.

**March: Conch Shell Blowing Contest** – shell blowers compete for the best and longest sounds.

**April: Indian Key Festival** – from Islamorada, visitors journey by boat to tour the little island destroyed by Indians in 1840.

**Late April: the Seven-Mile Bridge Run** – some 2,000 runners compete in a fun run across the famous bridge.

**Late April to early May: Conch Republic Celebrations** – Key West hosts a week-long party honoring the early settlers and reminding the State of Florida that it would rather be an independent nation.

**June: International Gay Arts Festival** – a showcase for the diverse artistic talents of the local gay community in Key West.

*Papa-look-alike contest*

**July 4: the Starspangled Event** – Marathon's waterfront celebration of Independence Day, with firework displays and a street party.

**Mid-July: Hemingway Days Festival** – a week-long event in tribute to Ernest Hemingway with Papa-look-alike contests, literary conferences and short-story competitions, with perhaps a bit of hard drinking as well.

**Mid-July: Lower Keys Underwater Music Festival** – boats equipped with underwater speakers broadcast classical and rock music across the reef at Looe Key Marine Sanctuary 6 miles (10km) south of Big Pine Key.

*Drag queens in competition*

**September: Key West Theater Festival** – along with readings and workshops on theater, a number of new plays are premiered.

**Mid-September: Women in Paradise Celebration** – a sailing, diving and dancing festival in honor of women, both gay and straight.

**Late October: Fantasy Fest** – an uninhibited Halloween celebration with a flamboyant tribute to gay pride that includes pet masquerades, tea dances and drag queen contests.

**Mid-November: Island Jubilee** – a two-day outdoor celebration of music, arts and crafts and local foods in Key Largo.

**Late November: Lower Keys Art Fair** – Big Pine Key hosts an outdoor art show featuring watercolors, pottery, jewelry, and iron sculpture by local and national artists.

# Food and Drink

*Opposite: How do you like your alligator ?*

While humdrum fast-food joints may mar the landscape of the Overseas Highway, the Florida Keys are in fact full of fine places to eat ranging from cozy, family-run little cafes to the sophisticated elegance of Key West's finest restaurants.

Surrounded by the sea, the focus here naturally is on fresh fish and seafood – grouper, snapper, shrimp, crab, conch and lobster. And if you see dolphin on the menu, don't worry: it is not the friendly kind you swim with, but a delicious spiny-finned fish which bears the same name. Some unusual freshwater specialties, such as sautéed frogs' legs and fried alligator tail, also show up on local menus.

*Seafood specialities*

Since south Florida is a veritable cornucopia of fresh produce that grows year-round, many modern chefs in the Keys incorporate citrus fruits, mangos, avocados, papayas, strawberries, coconuts and bananas into their nouvelle tropical cuisine. One local specialty in particular, Key lime pie, has become legendary: a creamy, tart-sweet yellow filling, made from eggs, milk and lime juice, packed into a thin graham cracker crust, Key lime pie is the perfect end to a perfect meal. With so many immigrants in the region, ethnic nuances have left their mark on the local diet, and now Cuban, Jamaican and Bahamian specialties are almost as commonplace as Key lime pie.

**63**

## Restaurant selections

The price categories of the following restaurants are based on the cost of a three course meal without wine. $$$ = over $25, $$ = $15-25, $ = under $15.

*Key lime pie*

*Key Largo*
**Caribbean Kitchen**, MM100.5, tel: 451-3042. Breakfast and Caribbean specialties including Creole omelets and cheese grits, 24-hours a day. $

**Mrs Mac's Kitchen**, MM99.4, tel: 451-3722. A locals' favorite with great burgers, fried fish and homemade pies. $

**The Fish House**, MM102.4, tel: 451-4665. Specialises in thick and spicy conch chowder and catch-of-the-day fish specials. $$

**Italian Fisherman**, MM104, tel: 451-4471. Italian seafood and classic pasta entrees. Outdoor seating and wonderful sunset views. $$

**Makoto**, MM99.5, tel: 451-7083. Japanese specialties – sushi, sashimi, teriyaki – using local fresh fish. $$

**Pilot House**, MM100, tel: 451-3142. Steaks and seafood with indoor and outdoor waterfront seating. $$

*Islamorada fish restaurant*

[Photograph of a seafood display]

*A surfeit of seafood*

*Islamorada*
**Manny and Isa's Kitchen**, tel: 664-5019. Authentic Cuban dishes such as roast pork, black bean soup and fried plantains. $

**Mexican Cantina**, MM81.5, tel: 664-3721. Traditional Mexican fajitas, quesadillas and guacamole. $

**Coral Grill**, MM83.5, tel: 664-4803. A sumptuous country-style buffet of prime rib, roast turkey and fried fish. $$

**Green Turtle Inn**, MM81, tel: 664-4918. A local institution since 1947, serving turtle steaks and fine seafood. $$

**Lorelei**, MM82, tel: 664-4656. Traditional conch fritters and Creole seafood specials. $$

**Whale Harbor**, MM83.5, tel: 664-4511. An all-you-can-eat seafood buffet featuring lobster, crab, shrimp and clams. $$

*Tempting the hungry*

*Big Pine Key*
**Island Reef**, MM31.3, tel: 872-2170. All-American comfort food such as chicken pot pie, Yankee pot roast and leg of lamb. $$

**Montego Bay**, MM30, tel: 872-3009. Spicy Jamaican dishes along with steaks, veal and pasta. $$

*Marathon*
**Stuffed Pig**, MM49, tel: 743-4059. A roadside cafe, serving breakfast and lunch only, but the huge portions of the best all-American barbecue pork will keep you going past dinner time. $

**Kelsey's**, MM48, tel: 743-9018. Award-winning continental cuisine with roast duck, prime ribs, fresh homemade bread, and luscious Key lime cheesecake and macadamia pie. $$

**The Cracked Conch,** MM49, tel: 743-2223. Conch burgers, conch steak, conch parmigiana. $
**Shuckers Raw Bar & Grill**, MM47.5, tel: 743-8686. Barbecued shrimp, fried oysters, seafood salads and crab soup. $
**Castaway**, MM48, tel: 743-6247. A locals' favorite featuring shrimp steamed in beer, roast chicken and hot bread dripping with honey. $$

*Sugarloaf Key*
**Mangrove Mama's**, MM20, tel: 745-3030. Terrific fish and natural foods in a 1960s hippie setting, housed in an old Caribbean shack. $$

*The Half Shell Raw Bar*

*Key West*
**El Cacique**, 125 Duval Street, tel: 294-4000. Cuban restaurant specialising in garlicky roast pork and stewed fish. Also open for breakfast. $
**El Siboney**, 900 Catherine Street, tel: 296-4184. One of the best Cuban restaurants in the Keys. $
**Gato Gordo**, 404 Southard Street, tel: 294-0888. Mexican dishes such as tostadas, burritos and cilantro rice amid hand-painted tiles and tropical art. $
**Half Shell Raw Bar**, Land's End Marina, tel: 295-7496. The big Eat-It-Raw sign out front says it all – clams, oysters and peel-your-own shrimps, in a former fish market, with a view of the fishing fleet. $
**Cafe Karumba**, 1215 Duval Street, tel: 296-2644. Contemporary Caribbean cuisine with one of the largest rum selections in the Keys. $$

*Save room for dessert*

**Finnegan's Wake**, 320 Grinnell Street, tel: 293-0222. Irish pub ambiance with Dublin pot pie, Irish stew, corned beef and cabbage, and Guinness, of course. $$
**Kelly's Caribbean Bar & Grill**, 301 Whitehead Street, tel: 293-8484. Island specialties such as tamarind chicken, mango chutney, coconut shrimp and home-brewed beer. $$

*Conch fritters stall*

**La-Te-Da Inn**, Duval Street, tel: 296-6706. Nouvelle cuisine in an elegant setting. $$
**Mangia Mangia**, 900 Southard Street, tel: 294-2469. It's worth the wait you may experience to try the home-made pasta. $$
**Louie's Backyard**, 700 Waddell Street, tel: 294-1061. Exceptional tropical cuisine with a romantic waterfront setting. $$$
**Cafe Marquesa**, 600 Flemming Street, tel: 292-1244. Fine 'Floribbean' cuisine, which means fresh seafood with exotic fruits and spices. $$$
**Dim Sum**, 613 Duval Street, tel: 294-6239. Enjoy Indian, Malay and Thai specialties in an elegant Asian setting. $$

# Nightlife

Dressing up for a night on the town in the Keys just involves putting on a clean shirt or dress. Even in the fanciest of nightclubs dress is casual, and evening entertainment usually revolves around drinking exotic cocktails and listening to live and loud reggae, calypso, rock, country or Latin music. The legal drinking age is 21, and bars and clubs do check identification.

*Tiki Bar*

*Brass Monkey blues*

66

## Nightclubs and bars

**Groucho's**, MM100, Key Largo. Live music and comedy acts.

**The Harbor Bar**, MM83, Islamorada. Live music in a rustic setting.

**Tiki in the Sky Bar**, MM84, Islamorada. Live reggae and rock in a bar perched above the water.

**Brass Monkey Lounge**, MM50, Marathon. A low-key locals' hangout.

**Hog's Breath Saloon**, 400 Fulton Street, Key West. Loud and rambunctious live entertainment.

**Sunset Pier Bar**, 0 Duval Street, Key West. Live music, just a few steps away from the Mallory Square sunset craziness.

**The Top Lounge**, 430 Duval Street, Key West. Generous drinks and panoramic views from the tallest building in Key West.

**Havana Docks Lounge**, 1 Duval Street, Key West. High-energy disco dance music.

## Theaters

**Red Barn Theater**, 319 Duval Street, Key West, tel: 296-9911. A professional 90-seat playhouse with dramas, musicals and comedies by local and national playwrights. Open December to June.

**Tennessee Williams Fine Arts Center**, 5901 Junior College Road, Stock Island, tel: 296-9081. A 490-seat theater dedicated to the playwright, featuring dramas, jazz and classical concerts, and dance presentations. Open all year.

**Waterfront Playhouse**, Mallory Square, Key West, tel: 296-9081. An 185-seat community theater, housed in a 19th-century wreckers' warehouse, presenting comedies and dramas. Open November to May.

## Cinemas

**Cobbs Theater**, Searstown Shopping Center, Key West, tel: 294-0000.

**Tavernier Town Twin Cinema**, MM91.5, Tavernier, tel: 852-9910.

**West Side Cinema**, MM51, Marathon, tel: 743-0288.

# Shopping

Although there are a scattering of upscale shopping centers throughout the Keys which offer designer clothing and fine jewelry, most of the must-take-it-home tourist shopping relates to the sea. Conch shells and white and pink mollusks, bigger than a hand, which sound like the sea when held to the ear, are abundant. Natural sponges, hand-rolled cigars, lotions and cosmetics made from the local aloe plant, and clothing in natural fabrics and bright tropical colors are also popular items, as are tiny bikinis and wide-brimmed hats.

*Teeny-weeny bikinis*

**The Shell Man**, MM106, Key Largo. Shells, of course.
**Caribbean Cigar Shop and Factory**, MM103, Key Largo. Huge selection of cigars.
**Josie's Junk Alley**, MM99, Key Largo. Good for browsing.
**Key West Aloe**, MM82, Islamorada. Perfumes, cosmetics, shampoos, etc.
**The Quay Shops**, MM54, Marathon. A wide selection of goods and gifts.
**Banana Boat Boutique**, 419 Duval Street, Key West. Hand-painted cotton clothes.
**Key West Kite Shop**, 409 Green Street, Key West. Great choice of kites and wind chimes.
**Key West Aloe**, 504 Green Street, Key West. Biggest selection of aloe products in the Keys.
**Hot Hats**, 613 Duval Street, Key West. All kinds of headgear.
**Key West Cigar Factory**, 3 Pirates Alley, Key West. Quality hand-rolled cigars and smoking accessories.
**Key West Hand Print Fabrics**, 201 Simonton Street, Key West. Ready-made clothes as well as fabrics.

*The Shell Man's selection*

*Key West Kite Shop*

*Preparing to dive*

## Active Vacations

Outdoor activities in the Florida Keys are almost always watersports. There are golf courses and bicycle paths, but when it comes to the feel of the sea on skin, few places in the US can compare. With an average surf temperature around 75°F (24°C), it's easy to see why.

### Sailing and windsurfing

Windsurfers and small sailboats can be rented from:
**Coral Reef Park Company**, Key Largo, tel: 451-1621.
**Caribbean Watersports**, Key Largo, tel: 852-4707.
**Tropical Sailboats**, Key West, tel: 294-2696.
**Sunset Watersports**, Key West, tel: 296-2554.

### Diving and snorkeling

Dozens of dive and snorkel shops that offer rental equipment are located on Overseas Highway throughout the Keys and in Key West. Some shops offer boat trips out to the reefs, others provide nautical maps and point out the best underwater spots in their areas. Scuba equipment is available only to qualified divers who have proof of scuba certification; but snorkels, masks and flippers can be rented by anyone. The following are a few reputable shops:

*Sharkey's Dive shop*

**American Diving Headquarters**, Key Largo, tel: 451-0037.
**Bud 'n' Mary's Marina and Dive Center**, Islamorada, tel: 664-2211.
**Captain's Corner**, Key West, tel: 296-8918.
**Florida Keys Dive Center**, Tavernier, tel: 852-4599.
**John Pennekamp Dive Center**, Key Largo, tel: 451 6325.
**Key West Dive Inc.**, Key West, tel: 294-7177.
**Reef Raiders**, Key West, tel: 294-3635.
**Sharkey's Dive Shop**, Key Largo, tel: 451-5533.
**Treasure Divers**, Islamorada, tel: 664-5111.

### Fishing

Fishing in the Keys can mean going out on an expensive, fully-rigged sport-fishing boat or just tossing a line off the side of a bridge. Either way, there are many equipment rental shops and professional guides available. Most boat shops will sell you a saltwater fishing license. For a printed list of professional fishing guides write to: Florida Keys Fishing Guides Association, PO Box 936, Islamorada, FL 33036.

Some local fishing operators are:
**Back Country Adventures**, Key Largo, tel: 451-1247.

*Fishing gear to rent*

*Book a dive trip here*

**Gulf Lady**, Islamorada, tel: 664-2626.
**Marathon Lady**, Marathon, tel: 743-5580.
**MV Florida Fish Finders**, Key West, tel: 296-0111.
**Strike Zone Charters**, Big Pine Key, tel: 872-9863.
**Yankee Fleet**, Key West, tel: 294-7009.

**69**

## Canoeing/kayaking

Equipment rental and guided tours are available from:
**Florida Bay Outfitters**, Key Largo, tel: 451-3018.
**Key West Rowing Club**, Key West, tel: 292-7984.
**Mosquito Coast Wildlife Tours**, Key West, tel: 294-7178.
**Reflections Kayak Nature Tours**, Big Pine Key, tel: 872-2896.

## Land sports

A few of the resorts in the Keys have their own private **golf courses** for guests, and there are also two public courses: Key Colony Beach Par-3 is a 9-hole course near Marathon, tel: 289-1533; and Key West Resort Golf Course is an 18-hole course on Stock Island, tel: 294-5232.

*Bikes for hire*

**Bicycling** is an easy sport in the Keys because the terrain is so flat. Rentals are available from:
**Adventure Rentals**, Key West, tel: 292-1666.
**Bicycle Center**, Key West, tel: 294-4556.
**KBC Bike Shop**, MM53, Marathon, tel: 289-1670.
**Key Largo Bikes**, tel: 451-1910.
**Pete's Bikes**, Islamorada, tel: 664-4567.

Some of the resorts in the Keys allow the public to play **tennis** on their private courts for a fee. In Key West there are two public no-fee tennis courts: Bayview Park, 1310 Truman Avenue; and Higgs County Beach, Atlantic Boulevard and White Street.

# Getting There

*Opposite: Stop in Key Largo*

## By air

Most air travelers get to the Keys via **Miami International Airport** (tel: 876-7077), from where they either rent a car or take one of the commuter flights into Marathon or Key West. Airport check-in time is one hour prior for domestic flights and two hours for international flights. The Fort Lauderdale International Airport is another option, and is about a 45-minute drive north of Miami. Airlines that service the Keys from Miami and Fort Lauderdale are: **American Eagle**, tel: 800-433-7300; **Gulfstream**, tel: 871-1200; and **Delta ComAir**, tel: 800-345-9822.

*Key West Airport*

## By car

Rental cars are available at Miami airport and at many locations throughout the city. Some offer packages whereby you can pick up a car in Miami, drive to Key West, then fly back to Miami. Rental vehicles range from slick convertibles to comfortable vans; prices vary, depending on the company and time of year. A major credit card is required in order to rent a car. Contact the following:

**Alamo**, tel: 800-327-9633
**Avis**, tel: 800-331-1212
**Budget**, tel: 800-525-0700
**Hertz**, tel: 800-654-3131
**National**, tel: 800-328-4567

71

If you're driving to the Keys from other parts of Florida, the main north-south routes are I-75, I-95 and the Florida Turnpike. Once in the Miami area, there are two routes to the Keys: the Florida Turnpike, which ends in Homestead, or I-95, which ends at the southern end of Miami and becomes US1. Both roads lead to the Overseas Highway, the only road through the Keys. Small green Mile Marker signs are posted along the highway, MM0 being Key West, the southernmost point. From Miami, it takes about one and a half hours to drive to Key Largo, and three hours to Key West.

*On the road*

## By rail and bus

Train services on **Amtrak** bring passengers as far south as Miami. Tel: 800-USA-RAIL.

The main bus line serving the Keys from Miami and other parts of the US is **Greyhound**, with eight scheduled stops between Miami and Key West, tel: 800-231-2222. Smaller bus services are also available from Miami: Super Shuttle, tel: 871-2000; Island Taxi, tel: 664-8181; and Airporter, tel: 800-830-3414.

## Getting Around

Not for hire

*Not for hire*

*Nipping through traffic*

### By car

Except for Key West, where walking and cycling are the most practical forms of transportation, getting around in the rest of the Keys usually requires a car (*see Getting There on page 71 for details of car rentals*). The speed limit on the Overseas Highway is 55mph (88kph), with lower speed limits posted in cities. Speed limits are strictly enforced by the police who often use radar to monitor drivers. For the most part, the Overseas Highway has just two lanes and passing is allowed only in the occasional passing zones which are clearly posted. The highway can be dangerous at night and when it is raining, and caution is advised. It is common practice for drivers to keep their headlights on even during daylight hours and it may be sensible to adopt this practice.

Florida law requires all traffic to stop while a school bus is loading or unloading children; motorcyclists must wear helmets and ride with their headlights on; drivers and front seat passengers must wear seat-belts. Florida law also allows drivers to make a right turn at a red light after stopping.

### Public transportation

Taxis are available in the Keys but they can't be hailed on a street corner, and almost always require a phone call in advance. Some choices include: Maxi-Taxi, tel: 294-2222; Yellow Cabs of Key West, tel: 294-2227; Pink Cabs, tel: 296-6666; Florida Keys Taxi, tel: 296-7777. The city of Key West operates two public bus routes around the island, tel: 292-8165, but there are no bus services in the rest of the Keys.

*Leisurely pedal taxi*

# Facts for the Visitor

## Tourist information

The main source for general information on travel to Florida is the **Florida Division of Tourism**, 126 West Van Buren Street, Tallahassee, FL 32399, tel: 904-487-1462. The following is a list of regional Keys information offices:

**Florida Keys & Key West Visitors Bureau**, PO Box 1147, Key West, FL 33041, tel: 800-FLA-KEYS, and 296-1552.

**Key Largo Chamber of Commerce**, MM106, 105950 Overseas Highway, Key Largo, FL 33037, tel: 451-1414, fax: 451-4726.

**Islamorada Chamber of Commerce**, MM82.5, PO Box 915, Islamorada, FL 33036, tel: 664-4503, fax: 664-4289.

**Marathon Chamber of Commerce**, MM48.7, 3330 Overseas Highway, Marathon, FL 33050, tel: 743-5417.

**Lower Keys Chamber of Commerce**, MM31, PO Box 511, Big Pine Key, FL 33043, tel: 872-2411.

**Key West Chamber of Commerce**, 402 Wall Street, Key West, FL 33040, tel: 294-2587.

**73**

## Public holidays

Most state and government offices, post offices and banks are closed on the following dates:

New Year's Day (January 1); Martin Luther King Day (3rd Monday in January); President's Day (3rd Monday in February); Memorial Day (last Monday in May); Independence Day (July 4); Labor Day (1st Monday in September); Columbus Day (2nd Monday in October); Veterans' Day (November 11); Thanksgiving (4th Thursday in November); Christmas Day (December 25).

*Enjoying public holidays*

## Opening times

Business offices are open Monday to Friday 9am–5pm. The majority of shops and grocery stores are open Monday to Saturday, 10am–9pm, Sunday, 10am–6pm. Most tourist attractions are open on public holidays.

*Sensible advice*

## Tax

The Monroe County sales tax is 7 percent, with an additional 4 percent bed tax levied on all hotel rooms.

## Alcohol

Drinking alcohol in vehicles is prohibited; all opened liquor bottles must be stored in the trunk. The legal drinking age is 21 and identification is often checked.

*Shellfish restaurant*

*Micky's Bar, Islamorada*

*Unmistakable public phones*

## Tipping

In most restaurants and bars, tips are included only on bills for large groups. Otherwise, the standard rate is between 15 and 20 percent. Taxi drivers expect the same. Airport or hotel porters expect $1 per bag.

## Credit cards and travelers' checks

Credit cards are accepted at most commercial establishments, as are travelers' checks, for which you must produce a passport or photo identification card. Toll-free numbers to report lost or stolen credit cards or travelers' checks are: Visa, tel: 800-336-8472; Mastercard, tel: 800-982-2181; American Express, tel: 800-874-0410. Automatic cash dispensing machines are located at airports, shopping centers and large hotels.

## Postal services

Post offices usually open Monday to Friday 9am–5pm, and Saturday 8am–noon. Offices are located in Key Largo, Islamorada, Marathon, Big Pine, Summerland and Key West. Stamps can be purchased at most pharmacies, supermarkets, and hotels. Overnight delivery service is available through the US Post Office, Federal Express and United Parcel Service.

## Telephone

There are public phones in gas stations, hotels, restaurants and shopping centers. The area code for the Keys and Miami is 305, but calling Miami from the Keys, or the Upper Keys from the Lower Keys, is considered long distance so you dial 1-305 plus the number. For calls outside the 305 area dial 1 + the area code + the number. For international direct dialing, dial the international access code 011, then the country code. For directory information dial 411; for operator assistance dial 0. All numbers listed in this book are in the 305 area except those prefixed with 800 which are toll-free.

## Health and emergencies
In case of an emergency, tel: 911 and ask for the police, fire service or ambulance. At public phones, no coins are needed to call this number.

## Security and crime
Because of the incidence of crimes involving tourists, travelers who drive in the Miami area are advised to use caution. A common tactic used by local criminals is to bump into the car in front of them and rob the driver when he or she stops to examine the damage. If such a thing happens, drive to the nearest well-lit and crowded area before getting out of the car. In the Keys there is little need to worry about car crime, although storing valuables in the trunk is a good precaution.

*Keeping the peace*

## Medical care
Emergency medical care can be obtained 24 hours a day from: Mariners Hospital, MM88.5, Tavernier, tel: 852-9222; Fisherman's Hospital, MM48.7, Marathon, tel: 743-5533; Florida Keys Memorial Hospital, MM5, Stock Island, tel: 294-5531. For emergencies requiring immediate attention or an ambulance, tel: 911. If dental care is needed, call the East Coast Dental Society for a referral, tel: 667-3467.

Major pharmacies are located in Key Largo, Islamorada, Tavernier, Marathon and Key West. Most are open from 9am to 9pm.

## Media
The local newspapers of the Keys include the *Key West Citizen*, *Keynoter*, *Island Life* and the *Island Navigator*. The *Miami Herald* publishes a Keys edition that contains area news. Foreign newspapers can be purchased at several newsstands in Key West.

*Catching up on the news*

## Time
The Keys, and most of Florida, operate on Eastern Standard Time which is five hours behind Greenwich Mean Time. From the last Sunday in April to the last Sunday in October the clocks are set one hour ahead.

## Electricity
Standard electrical sockets operate on 110 volts with 220-volt razor sockets available at many hotels. Adapters for European electrical appliances are available from most hotel concierges.

## Additional Facts for Overseas Visitors

### Travel documents
A valid passport and return airline ticket are required for all overseas visitors. Visas are not necessary unless you are planning to stay for longer than 90 days.

### Customs
Upon arrival foreigners entering the United States must declare all items they have brought into the country. There is no limit to the amount of money or travelers' checks a visitor may bring into or out of the country, but amounts over US$5,000 must be reported to the US Customs office.

The duty-free allowance is one liter of liquor and one carton of cigarettes. Flowers and fresh foods made from vegetable or animal products may not be brought into the US.

*Roll up!*

### Currency and exchange
Foreign currencies can be exchanged at Miami International Airport, at all banks and at most major hotels. US currency notes of all denominations are the same size and they are all green in color, so be careful at first that you do not get confused. When exchanging currency, it's a good idea to ask for a few dollars in quarters as these are needed for car toll booths, telephones and parking meters.

*Phoning home*

### Medical assistance
The medical facilities in Florida are excellent, but they do require hospital or doctors' fees to be paid in cash or by credit card, and costs can be very high. You are strongly advised to purchase a travel insurance policy from your travel agent at home before entering the United States.

Visitors from overseas should also be aware that a number of drugs that are commonly sold over the counter in most parts of Europe require a prescription in the United States. It is wise therefore to bring any kind of medication you may need for the duration of your trip or else you will incur medical fees as well as the inconvenience of contacting a doctor to supply you with the prescription.

(*Also see Health and emergencies section on page 75, for addresses of hospitals, and details of pharmacies and emergency dental care.*)

### Diplomatic representation
**UK**: The nearest British Consulate is in Miami, tel: 374-1522.

Key Largo waterfront hotel

## Where to Stay

From romantic inns to rustic campgrounds, the Keys have many accommodation options, ranging from honeymoon expensive to backpacking bargains. One thing to look out for, however, is proximity to the Overseas Highway, which can be noisy at night. A free guide to area accommodations is available from The Florida Keys & Key West Visitors Bureau (*see Tourist Information, page 73*). The list below is rated as follows: $$$=expensive, $$=moderate, $=budget.

*Cautionary motel sign*

*Sheraton Key Largo*

*Key Largo*
**Bay Harbour Lodge**, MM97.7, tel: 852-5695. A rustic, woodsy resort with tiki huts and a swimmable beach. $$
**Gilbert Motel**, MM107.9, tel: 451-1133. Modest but clean and comfortable. $
**Largo Lodge**, MM101.5, tel: 451-0424. Paradise can be reasonable, with a private beach and a kitchen in every room. $
**Neptune's Hideaway**, MM104.2, tel: 451-0357. Pretty pink cottages with a private beach. $$
**Sheraton Key Largo**, MM97, tel: 852-5553. A stylish yet natural spot with in-room Jacuzzis. $$$
**Sunset Cove Motel**, MM99.5, tel: 451-0705. Budget-priced dormitory-style rooms along with larger guest rooms. $

*Holiday Isle Resort*

*Islamorada*
**Cheeca Lodge**, MM82.5, tel: 245-3755. A large and elegant resort with golf, tennis, two pools and beach. $$$
**Harbor Lights Resort**, MM85, tel: 664-3611. Simple but pleasant with private pool. $$

**Bed & Breakfast of Islamorada**, MM81.1, tel: 664-9321. Offers a relaxing, hospitable and homey environment. $.

**Breezy Palms Resort**, MM80, tel: 664-2361. Casual atmosphere with a variety of room choices. $

**Chesapeake Resort**, MM83.5, tel: 664-4662. Tropical decor villas with saltwater lagoon and two freshwater pools. $$$

**Islander Motel**, MM82.1, tel: 664-2031. Family-friendly with saltwater pool and private terraces. $

**Plantation Yacht Harbor Resort**, MM87, tel: 852-2381. Modest rooms on a sprawling property with tennis courts and freshwater pool. $$

*Floating suites in Marathon*

*Faro Blanco Marine Resort*

### Marathon

**Banana Bay Resort**, MM49.5, tel: 743-3500. Ten secluded acres with Caribbean-style guest rooms. $$

**Bonefish Resort**, MM58, tel: 743-7107. Modest but friendly establishment with the hospitality of a bed-and-breakfast. $

**Faro Blanco Marine Resort**, MM48.5, tel: 743-9018. A selection of cottages, condominiums and houseboats, with beach. $$

**Golden Grouper Motel**, MM57.5, tel: 743-5285. Laid-back and rustic rooms far from the highway. $

**Hawks Cay Resort & Marina**, MM61, tel: 743-7000. A family resort which has 14 resident dolphins on the premises. $$$

**Sombrero Resort**, MM50, tel: 743-2250. Garden and waterfront suites with kitchens; also tennis courts and marina. $$

**Valhalla Beach Resort**, MM56.5 Marathon, tel: 289-0616. A quiet Atlantic-side spot with modest rooms and small beach. $

### Big Pine Key

**The Barnacle**, MM33, tel: 872-3298. A whimsical bed-and-breakfast with large rooms and stained-glass windows. $

**Casa Grande**, MM33, tel: 872-2015. A mix of Mediterranean and Mexican decor with spacious rooms. $

**Palmer's Place Cottages**, MM28.5, tel: 872-2157. Comfortable cottages with private terraces. $

### Key West

**Artist House**, 534 Eaton Street, tel: 296-3977. A sophisticated Victorian guest house, its rooms filled with antiques and good paintings. It also has a garden with a pond. $$$

**Caribbean House**, 226 Petronia Street, tel: 296-1600.

A casual-style guest house with a clientele that is mostly European. $

**Curry Mansion**, 511 Caroline Street, tel: 294-5349. A magnificent antique-filled mansion-turned-inn with a garden pool area. $$$

*Curry Mansion interior*

**Econo Lodge Resort**, 3820 North Roosevelt Boulevard, tel: 294-5511. A modest but very well maintained resort. $$

**Heron House**, 512 Simonton Street, tel: 294-9227. An historic inn with a brick courtyard and lush pool. $$

**Holiday Inn Beachside**, 3841 North Roosevelt Boulevard, tel: 294-2571. A modern facility with beautifully landscaped pool area. $$

**Key West International Hostel**, 718 South Street, tel: 296-5719. The cheapest place in Key West, with dormitory-style rooms. $

**Marriott's Casa Marina Resort**, 1500 Reynolds Street, tel: 296-3535. An historic, romantic property built in the 1920s, with a wide oceanfront beach. $$$

**The Pier House**, 1 Duval Street, tel: 296-4600. A prime waterfront resort with luxurious amenities. $$$

**79**

**Southernmost Motel**, 1319 Duval Street, tel: 296-6577. A well-located, 125-room property with a modern motel, two romantic inns, solarium and pool. $$

*Buckets and spades for sale*

## Camping
Full camping facilities with electricity, water and showers are available at:

**John Pennekamp Coral Reef State Park**, MM102, Key Largo, tel: 451-1202.

**Long Key State Recreation Area**, MM67, Long Key, tel: 664-4815.

**Bahia Honda State Recreation Area**, MM36, Big Pine Key, tel: 872-2353.

*John Pennekamp State Park*

# Index